FOR KING AND EMPIRE

THE CANADIANS AT ARRAS
and the
DROCOURT-QUEANT LINE
August-September 1918

A Social History and Battlefield Tour

by N. M. Christie

CEF BOOKS
1997

For King & Empire
Volume: V
The Canadians at Arras
August to September 1918

ISBN 1-896979-16-5

1. Military   2. First World War   3. Canada

Published by:
CEF BOOKS
P.O. Box 29123
3500 Fallowfield Road
Nepean, Ontario
K2J 4A9

Other books in this Series
Volume I: The Canadians at Ypres, 22nd-26th April 1915
Volume II: The Canadians on the Somme, September-November 1916
Volume III: The Canadians at Vimy, April 1917
Volume IV: The Canadians at Passchendaele, October-November 1917
Volume V: The Canadians at Arras and the Drocourt-Queant Line,
August-September 1918
Volume VI: The Canadians at the Canal-du-Nord and Cambrai, September-October 1918
Volume VII: The Canadians at Amiens, August 1918

Front cover picture: Detail of The Vimy Memorial, France. (Photo by N. Christie).

Back cover picture: The grave of Private Charles Robinson, of Sudbury, Ontario. Died of wounds received at Monchy, 26 August 1918. Age 19. (Photo by N.Christie).

Printed in Canada.

RENDEZVOUS

I have a rendezvous with Death
At some disputed barricade,
When Spring comes back with rustling shade.
And apple-blossoms fill the air-
I have a rendezvous with Death
When Spring brings back blue days and fair.

It may be he shall take my hand
And lead me into his dark land
And close my eyes and quench my breath-
It may be I shall pass him still.

I have a rendezvous with Death
On some scarred slope of battered hill,
When spring comes round again this year
And the first meadow-flowers appear.

God knows 'twere better to be deep
Pillowed in silk and scented down,
Where love throbs out in blissful sleep,
Pulse nigh to pulse, and breath to breath,
Where hushed awakenings are dear...
But I've a rendezvous with Death
At midnight in some flaming town,
When Spring trips north again this year,
And I to my pledged word am true,
I shall not fail that rendezvous.

Alan Seeger.
(1888-1916)

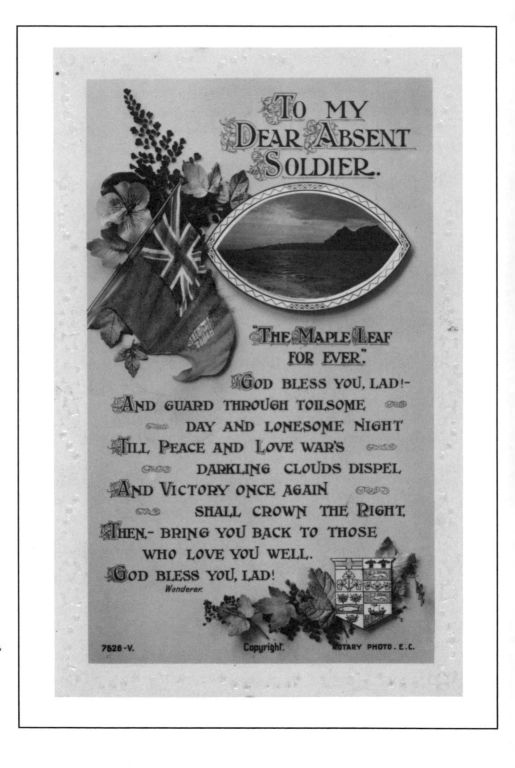

TABLE OF CONTENTS

The grave of Sgt. A. Knight, VC, in Dominion Cemetery.

INTRODUCTION
THE BATTLE OF ARRAS AND THE
DROCOURT-QUEANT LINE, August - September 1918

The Battle of Arras and the breaking of the Drocourt-Queant line was the greatest military achievement of the Great War. In 9 days of heavy fighting the men of the Canadian Corps broke through 5 successive German defensive lines and cracked the Drocourt-Queant line. Their constant pressure finally turned the northern flank of the impregnable Hindenburg line forcing the Germans to evacuate recently captured territory, from St. Quentin to Ypres in the North.

The tenacity of the Canadian attack, and its execution, whether as part of a large unit action or as small groups quickly re-organizing for a local attack, demoralized the German defenders. In their fight to the finish it was Canadian ingenuity, flexibility and courage that finally won the day.

The cost to Canada for this victory was enormous. Between August 26th and September 3rd, 1918 more than 11,000 Canadians were killed, wounded or missing.

The Battle of Arras and the breaking of the Drocourt-Queant line was the second huge Canadian victory in what became to be known as, "The Last Hundred Days," and was the crowning achievement of the Canadian Corps. "The Last Hundred Days" capped the progression of the Canadians; from 1915, as a force of primarily British-born Colonials, where they withstood the gas, through 1916 at Mount Sorrel and the Somme, where like so many others, they died in great numbers. At Vimy in 1917 the Canadian Corps first exhibited that efficiency and execution when they took the "Ridge." Passchendaele was a slaughterhouse but showed their will for victory, although at a terrible cost.

By 1918 the Canadians were confident if not cocky about themselves. They were held in reserve during the major German offensives along the British and French fronts and watched the German Army drive the Allies back, seemingly at will.

By the time the German onslaught was finally stopped they had nearly captured Amiens, and the capture of Paris and the Channel ports seemed within their grasp.

Finally it was the Canadian's turn and near Amiens on August 8th, 1918, attacking with the Australians, they drove back the Germans over 12 kilometres, marking their first victory.

The next attack was at Arras, and here they showed again their superiority over the Germans. After Arras, the Canadian Corps was exhausted but only 3 weeks later they struck again at the Canal-du-Nord and Cambrai once again driving the determined Germans back. Over the next month and a half they chased their enemy, capturing Denain, Valenciennes and Mons, on the last night of the war. They captured territory in days that would have taken months in 1916 or 1917.

Their battles of "The Last Hundred Days" were huge victories and the role of the Canadian Corps as the spearhead should never be forgotten.

For Canada the last three months were some of the worst in the war. In August, 4563 Canadians died, and in September 4548. Next to April 1917, these were the worst two 2 months of the war.

For the families, the death of their loved one; a father, a brother, a husband or a son, so close to the end of the war must have brought grief beyond words.

Today, in Canada, the names of Arras, Amiens, Cambrai, Drocourt-Queant and Canal-du-Nord are completely forgotten. The sacrifices of those young men do not even get a moment's memory. They are lost in time.

They do still live in the farming villages between Arras and Cambrai and in the farmers' fields. Their graves lie neatly, proudly displaying the Canadian Maple Leaf.

Today, the villages are much the same; small farming areas. There is no evidence of the Hindenburg line with the exception of a few pillboxes. Gone is the barbed wire, the reek of cordite and the noise of battle. But with a little thought you can imagine what it was like for our forefathers, and marvel at their success. They were truly great men.

I respectfully dedicate this book to the men of the Canadian Corps, who at Arras in 1918 won the greatest military victory of the war.

GETTING THERE

This guide recommends Arras as your centre of operations for visiting the Arras battlefields, which are within 10 kilometres of the town. The battlefield of Vimy 1917 is less than eight kilometres north.

Arras is used to accommodating tourists and provides the best facilities in the region. Tourist authorities can provide details on bed and breakfast facilities near the battlefields for a less-expensive alternative.

Arras is the capital of the Pas-de-Calais in northern France, 170 kilometres north of Paris and easily accessible from London. A two-hour drive to Dover, a 75-minute ferry ride or 35-minute Hovercraft journey to Calais, and a one-hour drive on the major Calais-to-Paris toll road will get you to Arras or you could take the rail link through the Channel Tunnel from London to Lille, which is 45 minutes northeast of Arras near the Belgian border. Arras is about 1.5 hours by road from Brussels. Check with the Tourist Board for details.

Rental cars are available in any of these cities and tourist offices can supply routes and details of hotels. In Arras, English is generally spoken in the main hotels. Otherwise very little English is spoken. Brush up on your French before going.

In France, stores close between noon and 2:00 p.m. always. Be sure to obtain film and other necessities before closing! Stopping for a long lunch is a strict and revered tradition in continental Europe. There are 3.5 French francs (1997) to a Canadian dollar. Currency and traveler's checks can be exchanged at any bank. Always visit the Tourism Office to obtain information on accommodation or events of interest.

WHAT TO BRING

Weather is very changeable in this part of Europe. Days can start sunny and change quickly to rain, hail or even a sprinkling of snow. Above all, be prepared for wet weather.

Other than the obvious passport, traveller's checks and appropriate clothing, bring the following to ensure a successful trip:

- a bottle opener and cork screw

- binoculars

- a camera (with 100 and 200 ASA film)

- a compass

- rubber boots

- Institut geographique national map numbers 2406 east Arras, 2506 west and 2507 Croiselles 1:25,000 (they can be obtained at most bookstores in Arras)

- Michelin map No. 53 (preferably the Commonwealth War Graves Commission overprint, showing all the cemeteries)

- reference books (do your research before departure)

ABOUT ARRAS

Although situated in the heart of the industrial north of France, Arras rests quietly and peacefully, with an air of grandeur and finesse reflected in its great white cobbled squares. No factory chimneys here, only the elegance of tradition which the city's inhabitants have fiercely held onto through thousands of years of captivity and terror. Badly damaged during the First World War, the inhabitants of the capital of Artois restored their incomparable monuments, the Grand'Place, place des Héros (Petite-Place), the rue de la Taillerie and the Town Hall in their original Flemish Gothic style, which make Arras one of the most beautiful towns in the north of France.

Of Roman origin, Arras was a stronghold in Julius Caesar's day. It was originally built on Baudimont Hill, east of the Crinchon Stream which runs through the town and called Atrebatum after a tribe which lived in the area, the Atrebates. Arras is a corruption of that name.

In the 5th century, during the reign of the Frankish king, Clovis I, Christianity was preached by Saint-Vaast, who created the diocese of Arras and was its first bishop. The most important abbey in the region was built in the 600s to honour the saint. A new town gradually emerged under the protection of this powerful monastery and eventually separated from the original construction by a continuous line of fortifications. By the 11th century, the two communities were quite independent of each other, each with its own form of government. The older Roman city on Baudimont Hill was the Cité of Arras and was under the jurisdiction of the bishop. The other, to the west, was the Ville proper and a dependency of the St. Vaast Abbey.

While the Ville grew steadily, the Cité gradually declined until the mid-18th century when it was incorporated in the Ville. Until Arras became part of the kingdom in France in the mid-17th century, the "Ville", as the capital of the County of Artois, successively belonged to the Counts of Flanders (850-1180), to the Counts of Artois (1180-1384), to the Dukes of Burgundy (1384-1492) and finally to the Kings of Spain (1492-1640).

The French kings often interfered in the affairs of Arras throughout this period. The town was besieged four times by the kings of

German prisoners passing through Arras, August 1918
(PUBLIC ARCHIVES OF CANADA PA-3076)

France in the 9th and 10th centuries. In the 14th century, Arras was torn by popular sedition. Under the Dukes of Burgundy, and especially under Philippe-le-Bon, the town's world-renowned cloth and tapestry industries enjoyed a period of great prosperity. Its Arrazi tapestries became famous.

Arras is also infamous for imprisoning Joan of Arc during October and November 1430.

When Louis XI tried to claim Artois in 1477, the Cité of Arras promptly opened its gates to the Royal Army, but the Ville refused to surrender and was only conquered in 1479, after a long siege. Furious at the people's resistance, Louis XI exiled all the inhabitants and brought in the "Ligeriens." Arras became Spanish and its name was changed to Franchise. A few months later, the people of Arras were allowed to return to their homes, and in 1483, its ancient name, armorial bearings and laws were restored.

The inhabitants of Arras resisted French domination for years following the incident with Louis XI. They opened their gates to the German and Burgundian troops of Austria in 1492, only to regret doing so when the Germans pillaged and rifled their valuables.

The Spanish-controlled city again came under the rule of the kings of France in the mid-17th century, when it fell after a long and bloody siege. The bombardments caused great damage to the abbey. A decade or so later, the town held out heroically against a Spanish invasion for 45 days.

Birth place of Augustin Robespierre, Arras was not spared during the Revolution. In 1793, Joseph Le Bon, sent there on a mission, organized the Terror. The guillotine was permanently erected in the Place de la Comédie. Travellers avoided Arras and the local merchants stopped doing business.

During the Great War, the Germans occupied Arras for only three days, September 6-9, 1914. But after their departure, the "Martyrdom of Arras" began. The Germans remained at the gates of the city until April 1917. Bombardment began October 6, 1914. Gunners fired ceaselessly on the military quarters and the two famous squares. The Hôtel de Ville, the Abbey of Saint Vaast and the Cathedral were burnt down, the belfry destroyed and by April 1917, Arras was completely in ruins. In March 1918, when the great German Offensive began, the bombardments broke out afresh, inhabitants were evacuated and by the end of August, the British drove the enemy out for good.

A visit to Arras should begin in the architecturally-unique Grand'Place, once an orchard belonging to the Abbey of Saint Vaast, and the Petite-Place. These squares have been bordered with gabled private houses and edged with stone columns and elliptical arches supporting vaulted galleries for hundreds of years.

Merchants once drew crowds of buyers to their stalls under the porticos of the squares and the famous tapestries of Arras were once made in the damp cellars under the galleries.

Bordering the west side of the Petite-Place is the Hôtel de Ville, above which rises the graceful silhouette of the belfry. Long the centre of town, the Petite-Place attracted the townspeople to public meetings, festivals and public executions.

Today, the tourist office is located at the Hôtel de Ville (21 51 26 95) and is open daily. From there, guided tours can be arranged of the underground tunnels beneath the town hall (35 minutes, year-round).

Arras was not spared by Allied bombing in the Second World War. A Canadian soldier surveys the ruined train station, September 1944.

(PUBLIC ARCHIVES OF CANADA PA-140196)

First used as cellars, the tunnels often served as shelters for the population during invasions and for the soldiers of the First World War. You can also visit the belfry.

Two-hour tours of the town are also offered by guide-lecturers of the National Association for Historical Sites and Buildings daily in July and August at 3:00 p.m. and Wednesdays and Saturdays in June and September at 3:00 p.m. Reserve at the tourist office.

The Abbey of Saint-Vaast shelters the rich collections of the Museum, and is a masterpiece of classical religious architecture.

Note, most museums in France are open 10:00 a.m. to noon and 2:00 to 6:00 p.m. and closed on Tuesdays. Sunday and winter hours may be reduced. Abbey tel. 21 71 26 43.

Arras is famous for its "cobalt blue" porcelain, first produced in the late 18th century. It is available in most tourist shops in the town centre.

Accommodation is not a problem in Arras. You may want to check out the following hotels:

Astoria, 10 place Foch, 62000 Arras, tel. 21 71 08 14

Hôtel Ibis, place Viviani, 62000 Arras, tel. 21 23 61 61

Mercure Hôtel (3-star), 58 boulevard Carnot, 62000 Arras, tel. 21 23 88 88

Hôtel Moderne, 1 boulevard Faidherbe, 62000 Arras, tel. 21 23 39 57

Ostel des 3 Luppars, 47 Grand'Place, 62000 Arras, tel. 21 07 41 41

Hôtel de l'Univers, 5 place Croix Rouge, 62000 Arras, tel. 21 71 34 01

Some eating establishments to consider are the restaurant at the Astoria which serves traditional French cuisine, tel. 21 71 29 78; or La Faisanderie, 45 Grand'Place (opposite 3 Luppars), tel. 21 48 20 76. As well, there is a variety of restaurants and cafés at the station square.

COMPONENTS OF THE CANADIAN EXPEDITIONARY FORCE

ARRAS 1918

1ST CANADIAN DIVISION

1st Infantry Brigade	2nd Infantry Brigade	3rd Infantry Brigade
1st Battalion (Western Ontario)	5th Battalion (Saskatchewan)	13th Battalion (Black Watch of Montreal)
2nd Battalion (Eastern Ontario)	7th Battalion (British Columbia)	14th Battalion (Royal Montreal Regiment)
3rd Battalion (Toronto Regiment)	8th Battalion (90th Rifles of Winnipeg)	15th Battalion (48th Highlanders of Toronto)
4th Battalion (Central Ontario)	10th Battalion (Alberta)	16th Battalion (Canadian Scottish)

2ND CANADIAN DIVISION

4th Infantry Brigade	5th Infantry Brigade	6th Infantry Brigade
18th Battalion (Western Ontario)	22nd Battalion (Canadien-français)	27th Battalion (City of Winnipeg)
19th Battalion (Central Ontario)	24th Battalion (Victoria Rifles of Montreal)	28th Battalion (Saskatchewan)
20th Battalion (Central Ontario)	25th Battalion (Nova Scotia)	29th Battalion (British Columbia)
21st Battalion (Eastern Ontario)	26th Battalion (New Brunswick)	31st Battalion (Alberta)

3RD CANADIAN DIVISION

7th Infantry Brigade	8th Infantry Brigade	9th Infantry Brigade
Royal Canadian Regiment (Nova Scotia)	1st Canadian Mounted Rifles (Saskatchewan)	43rd Battalion (Cameron Highlanders of Winnipeg)
Princess Patricia's Canadian Light Infantry (Eastern Ontario)	2nd Canadian Mounted Rifles (British Columbia)	52nd Battalion (New Ontario)
42nd Battalion (Black Watch of Montreal)	4th Canadian Mounted Rifles (Central Ontario)	58th Battalion (Central Ontario)
49th Battalion (Alberta)	5th Canadian Mounted Rifles (Quebec)	116th Battalion (Ontario County)

4TH CANADIAN DIVISION

10th Infantry Brigade	11th Infantry Brigade	12th Infantry Brigade
44th Battalion (Manitoba)	54th Battalion (Central Ontario)	38th Battalion (Eastern Ontario)
46th Battalion (Saskatchewan)	75th Battalion (Mississauga Horse)	72nd Battalion (Seaforth Highlanders of Vancouver)
47th Battalion (Western Ontario)	87th Battalion (Grenadier Guards of Montreal)	78th Battalion (Winnipeg Grenadiers)
50th Battalion (Alberta)	102nd Battalion (Central Ontario)	85th Battalion (Nova Scotia Highlanders)

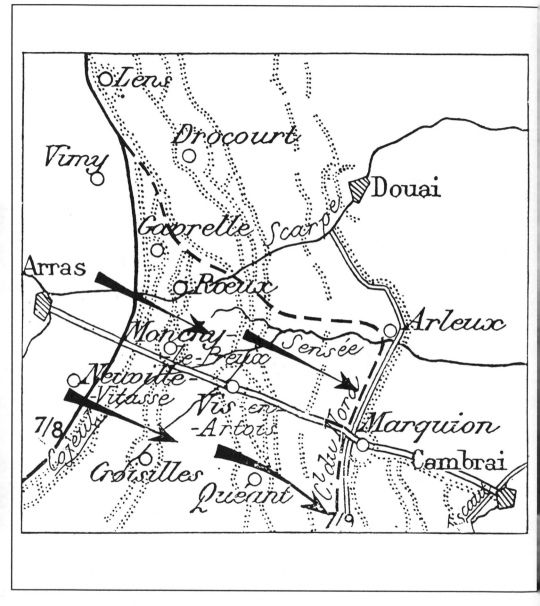

The Battle of Arras and the Drocourt-Queant line. August - September 1918.

The Battle of Arras and the Breaking of the Drocourt-Queant Line

Historical Overview

The Great War was characterized as a war of stalemate. Throughout 1915, 1916 and 1917 the armies sat opposed and neither side had the Manpower or strategy to break the other. 1918 brought changes to the style of warfare, it was to be the decisive year of the war and would involve great battles and mobility.

With the surrender of Russia in 1917 great numbers of experienced German troops were available for the Western front. The Allies knew the Germans would be coming in 1918 and anticipated the offensive by creating deeper defensive positions. They waited for the attack and on March 21st, 1918 the Germans smashed the British 5th Army at St. Quentin and drove quickly and deeply through the British defenses. The war of movement had begun. They next attacked the British 3rd Army near Cambrai and over the next week drove both British Armies back and inflicted more than 300,000 casualties on them. It was a rout.

The Canadians held their positions north of Arras and watched the German advance towards Amiens.

The British retreat continued until just east of Amiens when the line held and the impetus of the German attack petered out. In April the Germans attacked south of Ypres astride the Lys river and again drove back the British army. After a week's fighting, the line, comprised of French, British and Australian troops, held.

A third major German offensive was launched against British and French troops in the Champagne. For the Germans it was the same result. Initially they made great gains, but after several days the Allies fought the Germans to a standstill.

The German offensives had brought the Germans many prisoners and much territory but it left them exhausted and the 3 large, but weakly defended salients they had driven in the Western front left them vulnerable to counter-attacks.

The Canadians had remained in their lines near Arras or in reserve, almost observers of the horrific battles that raged around them. Their lack of action lead some to call them, not the proud Canadian Corps, but the Salvation Army!

The German Army was now overexposed and on July 18th, 1918 the French counter-attacked at Compiegne and won a large and easy victory.

Under a shroud of secrecy the Canadian Corps was moved into positions near Amiens. On August 8th, 1918 they attacked. The Germans were driven back 12 kilometres and 6 more on the following day before resistance stiffened. In mid-August the Canadians were brought back to Arras where they would make their second strike of "The Last Hundred Days."

The Battle of Arras 1918

The Corps was euphoric after the victory at Amiens but the task before them was formidable. Their objective was to break the major German defenses, a series of deep trench systems well protected with barbed wire, which made up the northern hinge of the Hindenburg line.

Unlike Amiens, the German positions were well constructed, strategically placed and protected by belts and belts of barbed wire. These defenses would not burst like a bubble. This was to be a hammer and anvil battle. The strategic value of the positions would also ensure the Germans would put up a stiff fight. If these positions fell the whole defensive position of the Hindenburg line could be outflanked. They also protected Cambrai, an important German transport and supply centre. The main German systems opposite the Canadians ran roughly north-south ending at the Scarpe river. The Canadian plan was to attack with the 3rd Division from the Arras-Cambrai road to the Scarpe river. The 2nd (British Columbia) and 4th (Toronto) Canadian Mounted Rifles would attack from the valley near Feuchy through the German front lines and up Orange Hill, a second German position. The assault would then be resumed by the 1st CMR (Saskatchewan) and together with the 5th CMR would capture the well-defended, village on the mound, Monchy-le-Preux. Other battalions of the 3rd Division, the 116th and 58th (Central Ontario), 52nd (Northern Ontario) and 43rd (Cameron Highlanders of Winnipeg) would carry on to capture the Fresnes-Rouvroy line, the last major defensive works blocking the true objective, the Drocourt-Queant line. The 51st Imperial Division was assigned the role of protecting the Canadian flank north of the Scarpe River by keeping up with the Canadian advance.

The Second Canadian Division was to advance from the outskirts of Tilloy-les-Mofflaines, driving south of the Arras-Cambrai road. From north to south, the 20th (Central Ontario), 21st (Eastern Ontario), and 27th (City of Winnipeg) battalions would attack in the first wave. The 28th (Saskatchewan) would then join the attack. They were to capture the positions surrounding the villages of Wancourt and Guemappe. The 18th (Western Ontario) would capture Guemappe village and the 19th and 20th (Central Ontario) battalions would push to Vis-en-Artois and the Fresnes-Rouvroy line. The other battalions of the Second Division, the 22nd (Canadien-francais), 24th (Victoria Rifles of Montreal) and the 26th (New Brunswick) battalions would capture Cherisy, the valley of the Sensee River and break into the Fresnes-Rouvroy line.

In the darkness, at 3 a.m. August 26th, 1918 the Battle commenced. On the 3rd Division front the CMR battalions were quickly all over the Germans. Orange Hill fell and by 7:40 a.m. Monchy was in Canadian hands. During the attack just north of the Arras-Cambrai road, Lieutenant Charles S. Rutherford MC, MM, of the 5th CMR single-handedly captured several machine guns and ensured that the advance would continue. He was awarded the Victoria Cross for his bravery.

The 3rd Division attack continued due east, with the 49th (Edmonton Regiment), Royal Canadian Regiment, Princess Patricia's Canadian Light Infantry and the 42nd (Black Watch of Montreal) battalions. By nightfall they were still a long way from the Fresnes-Rouvroy line. The attack would be renewed the next day.

August 26th had also gone well with the 2nd Division. All units had pushed forward, capturing Guemappe and Wancourt, stopping their advance on the heights east of the village.

On August 27th, 1918 the attack was renewed by both Divisions but opposition had stiffened. The 3rd Division pushed forward against the positions in front of the Fresnes-Rouvroy line, fighting furiously to capture Jigsaw Wood, the Bois du Sart and the Bois du Vert. The 2nd CMR and the 43rd Battalion captured Vis-en-Artois. No one had penetrated the Fresnes-Rouvroy line.

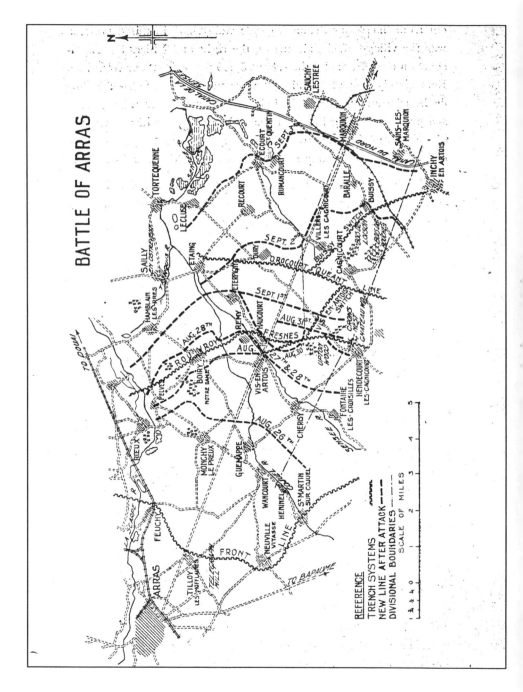

The 27th was a terrible day for the 2nd Division. After an initial success in capturing Cherisy and advancing across the Sensee River, German fire from the heights at Upton Wood and from the Fresnes-Rouvroy line stopped the advance. South of Vis-en-Artois the German trench systems also prevented the men from advancing. When nightfall came they were still too far away to launch a direct attack on the Fresnes-Rouvroy line and worse, they were opposed by belts of uncut barbed wire.

At 11 a.m. on August 28th, 1918 the 3rd Division launched a 6 battalion attack on the Fresnes-Rouvroy line. In heavy fighting the 58th and 52nd battalions broke into the village of Boiry-Notre Dame. The 4th and 5th CMR also broke the line and captured Remy and Haucourt. The German positions north of the Arras-Cambrai road were precarious. But south of the road the Germans smashed the advances of the 2nd Division. Blocked by barbed-wire and heavy fire from Upton Wood and Ocean Works the 2nd Division advance little for very heavy losses. The courage of the Second Division men was exceptional and every battalion suffered enormous losses. Lieutenant Colonel William Clark-Kennedy led his men, although severely wounded, for the duration of the disaster of August 27-28. He was awarded the Victoria Cross.

The attack of the Canadian Corps was behind schedule; the German resistance had been tougher than expected. But the attack had to continue. The decimated battalions of the 2nd Division were relieved by the 1st Division on the night of August 28th/29th, 1918. The 1st Division, the "Old Red Patch" had a great reputation of success even by Canadian Corps standards and they were put to a severe test at Upton Wood.

Their objective was to capture the Fresnes-Rouvroy line, the Vis-en-Artois Switch system which connected it to the Drocourt-Queant line, and the German positions on the heights at Upton Wood. On August 29th, 1918 in a brilliant action, the men of the 1st (Western Ontario) and the 2nd (Eastern Ontario) Battalions broke into the trench system, but instead of attacking east they wheeled north and attacked down the trench system, catching the Germans by surprise. The 2nd Battalion linked up with the 3rd (Toronto Regiment) and 8th (Black Devils of Winnipeg) at the Vis-en-Artois Switch. They were reinforced by the 4th Division's 72nd (Seaforth Highlanders of Vancouver), 38th (Ottawa) and the 85th (Nova

Belts of barbed wire protecting the Hindenburg line.
(PUBLIC ARCHIVES OF CANADA PA-3280)

Scotia Highlanders) Battalions and pushed the Germans eastward. The Germans fought tenaciously and over the next 3 days counter-attacked the Canadians, often regaining some lost ground only to lose it later. In one action the Germans had broken into the 38th Battalion's position near Haucourt. Private C.J.P. Nunney, DCM, MM, went up to the positions encouraging his beleaguered comrades to resist the attack. He continued the same on Mont Dury and by setting a fearless example greatly contributed to the success of the operation. He was then mortally wounded.

North of the Arras-Cambrai road, Canadian and British units advanced closer to jump-off positions that would be used in the next phase of the attack - the capture of the Drocourt-Queant line.

On August 31st and September 1st, the 1st Division fought to not only advance to a better jump-off position, but to retain their current position. At Upton Wood there was particularly heavy fighting but nonetheless the 15th (48th Highlanders of Toronto) not only fought off the counter-attacks but attacked to capture the critical position of the Crow's Nest, south-east of Upton Wood. It was an impressive feat.

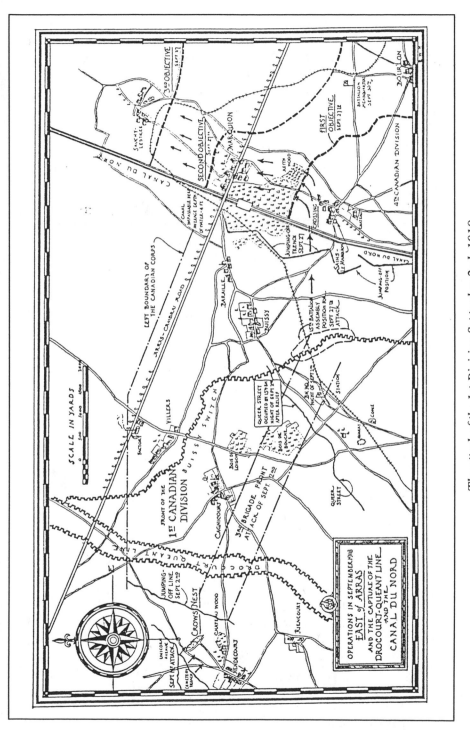

The attack of the 1st Division September 2nd, 1918

With fighting still going on the Canadian Corps Commander, Sir Arthur Currie ordered the attack on the D-Q line. The plan was for 5 Battalions of the 4th Division to attack the D-Q line at Mont Dury and Dury village. They would be attacking the formidable position from the shallow valley between Haucourt and Dury. The 1st Division would assault the D-Q line from their existing positions, capture both the front and support trench systems and push into the Buissy switch and drive for the Canal-du-Nord.

The 4th Division launched their attack at 5 a.m. on September 2nd, 1918. They had initial success with the 50th (Alberta), and 46th (Saskatchewan) Battalions breaking into Dury village but they could not push the Germans out. South of Dury, on Mont Dury, the 75th (Mississauga Horse), 87th (Montreal Grenadier Guards), 85th and 38th Battalions were cut to shreds by German machine-guns strategically placed south of the village, particularly in the sunken road that ran from Dury to the Arras-Cambrai road. Reinforcing Battalions, the 78th (Winnipeg Grenadiers) and 54th (Central Ontario) Battalions only added to disaster on Mont Dury.

Two Victoria Crosses were won there. Captain Bellenden Hutcheson, the Medical Officer of the 75th Battalion, and Private John Young of the 87th were awarded the VC for their tending of wounded under heavy fire. The only Battalion of the 4th Division to succeed that day was the 72nd. Their attack kept pace with the advancing 1st Division to the south and without their success their comrades on Mont Dury would have suffered even more.

The 1st Division attacked with the 7th (British Columbia), 13th (Black Watch of Montreal) and the 16th (Canadian Scottish) Battalions. The attack of the 13th and 16th was immediately successful, breaking through the D-Q line and pushing towards the Buissy Switch, taking many prisoners. Their assault came under heavy fire from Cagnicourt but they completed their task. The 16th Battalion won two Victoria Crosses this day; one to their Lieutenant Colonel, Cy Peck and the other to Corporal William Metcalf.

The attack of the 7th Battalion had also been successful and in no small way due to the actions of Private William Rayfield who captured a machine gun, a length of trench, 30 prisoners, and killed snipers. The 7th's attack was continued by the 10th (Alberta) Battalion who immediately ran into problems at the village of

Allan Reginald MacKedie
Lieutenant
18th West Ontario Battalion

Killed in action August 28th, 1918. Born at Montreal, December 18th, 1897. Son of John and Charlotte MacKedie of Montreal. Educated at Westmount Academy.

Enlisted at Vancouver in 1915 and transferred to the 18th Battalion: promoted Captain. Severely wounded in the arm, shoulder and chest at Dickebusch in July 1916.

During operations against the Fresnes-Rouvroy line, on August 28th, 1918, near Vis-en-Artois, his company was attacking a machine gun position when he was shot by a sniper and killed. He is buried in Vis-en-Artois British Cemetery.

Reay MacKay
Captain
26th (New Brunswick) Battalion

Killed in action August 27, 1918. Born at St. John, New Brunswick, May 14th, 1895. He was the son of Malcolm and Susan MacKay of Rothesay, New Brunswick.

In August 1915 he was appointed Lieutenant in the 64th Battalion, then transferred to the 26th Battalion.

On August 27th, 1918 as the Captain in command of his company during operations north-west of Cherisy he was instantly killed by the direct hit of a large enemy shell. His body was never recovered and he is commemorated by name only on the Vimy Memorial.

Villers-lez-Cagnicourt. The village had been built into the defensive works of the Buissy Switch and held up the 10th's attack. Again the actions of a single man changed the momentum of the battle. Sergeant Arthur Knight led a section of bombers and single-handedly bayonetted several machine gunners, and trench mortar crews and captured 20 Germans. Knight was mortally wounded later in the action.

As nightfall arrived the men of the 4th Division were still trapped on Mont Dury and many men of the 1st Division were hanging on in the Buissy switch. Both knew their positions were precarious and feared what the morning of September 3rd, 1918 would bring. At dawn, patrols were sent out but the Germans could not be found. After all the fighting, and after 11,000 casualties, the battle was over. The Drocourt-Queant line was captured and the Canadians had won in the showdown against a tenacious enemy. The Germans had blinked.

TOUR INTINERY
Duration 6.5 hours

Point 1:   *Tilloy Bunkers*

Point 2:   *Wancourt Tower*

Point 3:   *Sun Quarry Cemetery*

Point 4:   *Fresnes-Rouvroy line and the Vis-en Artois Switch.*

Point 5:   *Upton Wood*

Point 6:   *Dominion Cemetery*

Point 7:   *Dury Canadian Memorial*

Point 8:   *Dury Crucifix Cemetery*

Point 9:   *Buissy Switch*

Point 10:   *Fresnes-Rouvroy line at Boiry-Notre Dame*

Point 11:   *Orange Hill Cemetery*

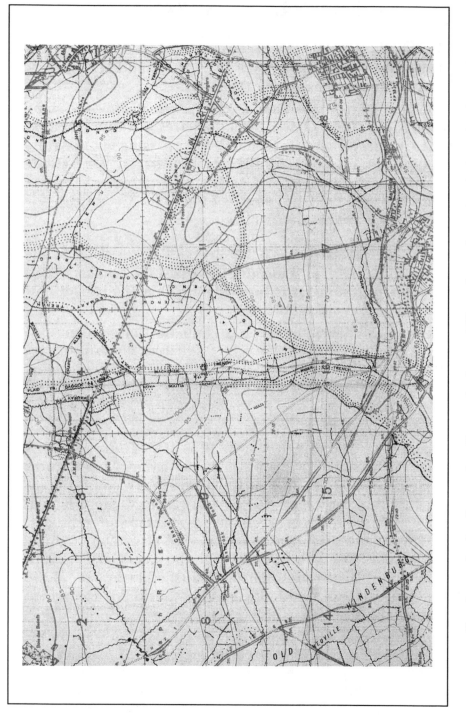

Trench map showing German front line trenches between Tilloy and Monchy, cutting the Arras-Cambrai road.

THE BATTLE OF ARRAS 1918

THE TOUR

Unlike the Canadian battles of 1915, 1916 and 1917, the battles of 1918 involve considerable distances, so be prepared to drive.

The tour starts in the Grande Place, Arras. Follow the signs to CAMBRAI (D939), after 3-4 kilometres a traffic circle is reached, continue towards Cambrai. After passing out of Arras, the village of Tilloy-les-Mofflaines appears on your right. Essentially the whole battle of Arras and the Drocourt-Queant line took place north and south of the Arras-Cambrai road. Cambrai is 32 kms SE of Arras.

At Tilloy-les-Mofflaines turn right into the village centre; continue until the sign for Tilloy British Cemetery. Turn left and follow the D37E to Wancourt. Drive past the cemetery, stop after 1 km on the heights marked with remains of German bunkers on either side of the road.

Tilloy-les-Mofflaines was captured from the Germans on April 9th, 1917. In the German March 1918 Offensive the British front line stabilized a few kilometres, east of Tilloy.

Point 1: Tilloy Bunkers

From this vantage point looking north you can see virtually all the battlefield of the 26th August 1918. This is the southern boundary of the Canadian Corps. To the north you can see Orange Hill, Monchy-le-Preux and on the main Arras-Cambrai road, Chapel Hill and just west of the rise, Feuchy Chapel British Cemetery. In the fields between the point where you stand and the Arras-Cambrai road, the 4th and 6th Canadian Infantry Brigades attacked successfully through the main German front lines and pushed ahead capturing Chapel Hill (the hill on the Arras-Cambrai road) and closing with the second line of German defences.

Return to your car and continue on the D37E to Wancourt.

After roughly one kilometre pass Tigris Lane Cemetery and after 700 metres pass Hibers Trench Cemetery. Enter Wancourt and pass straight through to Wancourt British Cemetery. This is a small road but continue up the ridge past Wancourt British

Cemetery (on your right) and over the rise. Four hundred metres past Wancourt British Cemetery, you reach the remains of Wancourt Tower and a German bunker on your right. Stop at the remains of the tower (it is a junction with a small road going north to Guemappe village).

Point 2: Wancourt Tower

Looking north you can see the territory gained by the 3rd Division on the 26th. Monchy-le-Preux is clearly visible on its mound. The Canadians had captured it and pushed just east on the 26th. The Bois du Vert, Boiry-Notre-Dame, Vis-en-Artois are clearly visible and were the objective for the 3rd Division on the 27th. The 2nd Division were to breech the Defensive lines running north-south in front of Cherisy and drive through the village and break into the main Fresnes- Rouvroy line, 1.5 kms east of the village. The attack jumped-off from this position and was made by the 26th (New Brunswick), 24th (Victoria Rifles of Montreal) and the 22nd Van Doos (Quebec).

Just south of the Arras-Cambrai road, the 19th (Central Ontario), 18th (Western Ontario) were to attack towards Vis-en-Artois. The church can be seen north-east of where you stand.

The 22nd and 24th Battalions jumped off from where you are standing. They met heavy resistance from the trenches in front of Cherisy. (The Cherisy church steeple can be seen due east). By noon the Germans positions were taken and the Canadians advanced quickly through Cherisy and into the valley of the Sensee River (more of a creek) and onto the heights east of the village.

The balance of the 2nd Division's attack had also gone well with the 18th and 19th Battalions, supported by the 20th (Central Ontario), and the 21st (Eastern Ontario) Battalions making gains into the heavily defended village of Vis-en-Artois.

To the north of the Arras-Cambrai road, the 43rd (Cameron Highlanders of Winnipeg) and the 2nd CMR captured German positions north of Vis-en-Artois.

Although the 27th had started well for the 2nd Division, the Battalions, weakened by heavy losses still had to attack the Fresnes-Rouvroy line running south of Vis-en-Artois. Against the heavily fortified heights and with depleted resources success was unlikely.

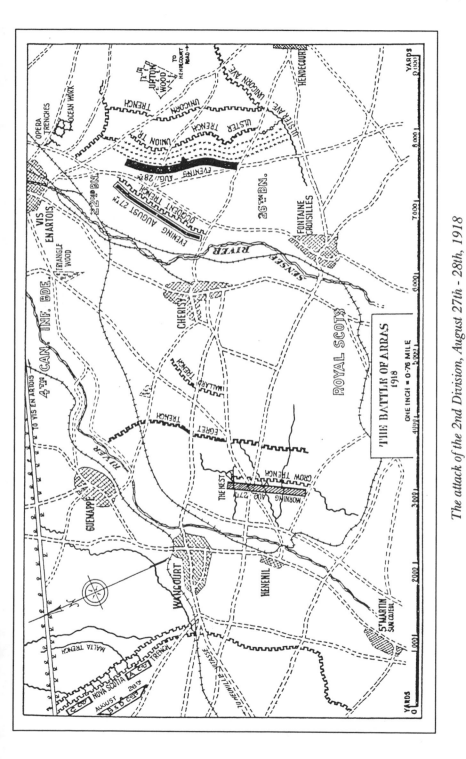

The attack of the 2nd Division, August 27th - 28th, 1918

View of Wancourt village and Monchy-le-Preux, the village in the background, from Wancourt ridge.

(PHOTO: N. CHRISTIE)

Return to your car and turn left on the small-paved road beside the ruins of the Wancourt Tower. Continue until the road meets the D38 after 800 metres. The road becomes windy as you drive into the Cojeul River valley. The terrain you have just crossed was captured by the 18th Battalion on the 26th August 1918. Turn right on the D38 towards Cherisy, follow the road into the village and pass through following the signs to Sun Quarry and Quebec Cemeteries. After 900 metres Sun Quarry Cemetery appears on your left. Stop at Sun Quarry Cemetery.

Point 3: Sun Quarry Cemetery

Looking back to Cherisy you can observe the village and the ground crossed by the 26th, 24th and 22nd Battalions on the 27th August. They advanced over the Sensee River (the creek you drove over 300 metres east of the village), and captured some German machine gun positions on the eastern river bank. Their objective now was the Fresnes-Rouvroy line, running north-south roughly 1 km east of you. The units of the 2nd Division attacked the German positions in front of the Fresnes-Rouvroy line and managed to capture these advanced positions 1 km north of Sun Quarry. However the losses of the 27th had been too severe and the Battalions were too disorganised to continue the attack. They also had encountered much uncut barbed wire and continuous firing from the German positions at Upton Wood made the advance impossible. The men of the 2nd Division were spread out from Sun Quarry Cemetery to Vis-en-Artois, in shell holes and captured trenches, seeking cover as they could. From these positions, the 2nd Division prepared for the assault on the Fresnes-Rouvroy Line, planned for the next morning, 28th August 1918.

Return to your car and continue on the road to the village of Hendecourt-les-Cagnicourt. After 1 km you cross the place where the main Fresnes-Rouvroy line would have intersected the road. This area was the responsibility of the British troops covering the right of the Canadian Corps.

The large wood to your left is Upton Wood (Bois d'Hendecourt) and was a heavily fortified. It covered the approaches to the Fresnes-Rouvroy line and provided enough artillery and machine-gun fire to stop any attack. The 2nd Division would find out the value of this position on the 28th August.

At Hendecourt turn left, continue through the village on the D956. On the outskirts of the village the road forks at a Calvary. The right leads to Dury on the D956. <u>Take the left fork</u>. Continue on the small, paved road past Upton Wood on your right and for 1 km north of the wood. As the road starts to descend towards the village of Vis-en-Artois, stop.

Point 4: The Fresnes-Rouvroy line and the Vis-en-Artois Switch

To orientate your position; the view north and west gives a clear view of Monchy, Bois du Vert, Boiry-Notre-Dame, Vis-en-Artois. South-west you see Cherisy village and the 2 trees east of the village mark Sun Quarry Cemetery. Due west 1 kilometre you can see Quebec Cemetery, the approximate line reached by the 2nd Division on the 27th. Looking south Upton Wood is clearly visible and its commanding position is evident. Looking north-east the white water tower in the village of Dury is visible (Dury was just inside the Drocourt-Queant position). South of Dury, on the Arras-

Canadian dead awaiting burial in Windmill British Cemetery, Monchy

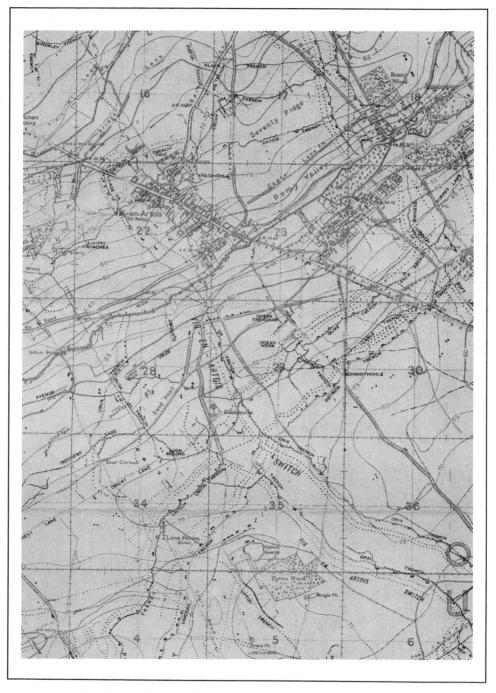

Trench map showing the German trench systems south of Vis-en Artois.

Cambrai road is the Canadian Memorial Park. Dury Mill Cemetery is just left of the park out on the ridge. This was the Drocourt-Queant line and the next Canadian objective after the Fresnes-Rouvroy line was taken.

The Fresnes-Rouvroy line ran north-south from Vis-en-Artois, 200 metres due west of you, and 1 km west of Hendecourt-les-Cagnicourt. The trench systems, Fresnes-Rouvroy and the Vis-en-Artois Switch met 800 metres north along the road you are now on. North-east of the junction and just south of the Arras-Cambrai road were the heavily fortified positions of Ocean Works and Opera trench connecting the north part of the Fresnes-Rouvroy line with the south. The position sitting less than 1 km north of you was formidable and it was against these systems the attack of the 28th was crushed.

The plan for the 28th was for the 2nd Division to continue its attack against those above-stated positions. North of the Arras-Cambrai road the 3rd Division would break the northern part of the line and push on to St. Servins Farm, east of Haucourt (It is visible from where you stand. It is the large isolated farm north-east of you and due east of the village of Haucourt). The objective of capturing these postitions was to secure a jumping off position 600 metres west of the Drocourt-Queant line.

From their positions west of you, the 2nd Division attack commenced at 12:30 p.m. It immediately ran into trouble against uncut barbed wire and heavy machine-gun and artillery fire. The 22nd, the 24th and the 26th courageously attacked through the wire but were unable to advance. The 22nd attacked just north of you and in the action lost all officers and 460 men. Amongst the officers put out of action was Georges Vanier[1], the future Governor-General of Canada. Vanier was shot through the ribs and as he was being attended to a shell exploded next to him, shattering his right knee and killing the stretcher-bearer. He was evacuated and his right leg was amputated at a Casualty Clearing Station the next day. Lt.Col. Clark-Kennedy[2], the Commanding Officer of the 24th was wounded early in the day but refused to be evacuated. He con-

---

[1] Georges Phileas Vanier; born Montreal, Quebec, April 23, 1888; died Ottawa, March 5, 1967.
[2] William Hew Clark-Kennedy; born Dunsky, Scotland, March 3, 1879; died Montreal, October 25, 1961.

Canadians in the ruins of Boiry-Notre Dame.

(PUBLIC ARCHIVES OF CANADA PA-4508)

The ruins of Vis-en-Artois.

(PUBLIC ARCHIVES OF CANADA PA-4436)

tinuously assisted his men and when realizing they could do no more established a defensive position about 100 metres closer from where they had started that morning. His bravery won Clark-Kennedy the Victoria Cross. Lieutenant Colonel Archibald McKenzie of the 26th Battalion was in an advanced position encouraging his men forward when he was killed by machine-gun fire.

Many of the men killed in this action are buried in Quebec Cemetery. It's name was taken due to the large numbers of the 24th and 22nd, both from Quebec, buried there. Lt.Col. McKenzie is buried in Wancourt British Cemetery with many of his men.

The 2nd Division had shot its bolt and were relieved by the 1st Canadian Division on the night of the 28-29th August 1918. When the 1st Division entered the Sensee River Valley they found a veritable graveyard of Canadian soldiers awaiting burial. The battle, so successful on the 26th, had become by the 27th and 28th a fight to the death. The Germans were fully aware of the importance of the lines and were not hesitating in sending reserves to stem the Canadian onslaught. The plan for the 1st Division was to crack the Fresnes-Rouvroy line and the Vis-en-Artois Switch. To do so Upton Wood would have to fall. 29th August 1918 passed quietly but on the 30th August the 1st Division launched a brilliant attack. At 4:40 am from the area of Sun Quarry Cemetery the 1st (Western Ontario) and 2nd (Eastern Ontario) battalions attacked towards Hendecourt and entered the German trenches. After capturing the front line they attacked down the trench clearing the German garrison from the south. The 3rd Battalion (Toronto Regiment) attacked the junction of the Fresnes-Rouvroy/Vis-en-Artois Switch and linked-up with the 2nd. The 1st Battalion continued its attack and captured the central German position of Upton Wood. The Germans counter-attacked fiercely to regain these important positions and although making some inroads could not recapture them. The 3rd Battalion fought for 5 hours to clear the junction of the main lines but could not capture Ocean Works and Opera trenches, south-east of Vis-en-Artois village.

On the 31st August 1918, the 8th (Black Devils of Winnipeg) Battalion finally captured Ocean Works. The Germans counter-attacked fiercely but neither side could improve their positions.

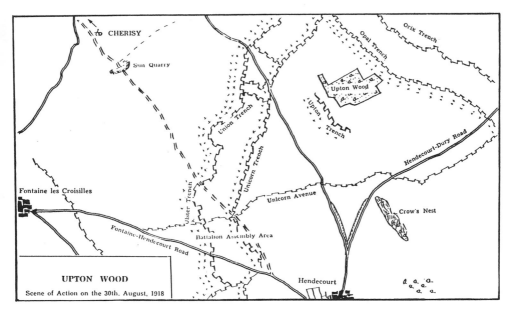

Upton Wood, August - September 1918

Canadian soldiers moving up, through a German barrage east of Arras, September 1918.

This ferocious action all took place within your view. It was a tenacious battle to hold these critical trenches.

At this point the Battle of Arras links with the capture of the main German line, the Drocourt-Queant line.

Return to your car and return to Hendecourt-les-Cagnicourt. At the Calvary fork turn left for DURY. After roughly 1 km turn left when you see the sign for Upton Wood Cemetery. At the cemetery, stop.

Point 5: The Drocourt-Queant line/Upton Wood/The Crows Nest

From where you stand, looking North you can see the Village of Dury, the Canadian Memorial Park and Dury Mill Cemetery. Due east Dominion Cemetery can be seen the open fields. The Drocourt-Queant line ran west of Dury in a north-south direction, passing through Dominion Cemetery and continuing on to Queant. The D-Q support line ran parallel and roughly 1 km east of the main line. The Buissy Switch ran south-east from the D-Q line west of Dury across the main Arras-Cambrai road (at the Canadian Monument Park), south-west of the village of Villers-les-Cagnicourt and the village of Buissy. It joined the main Hindenburg position at Inchy-en-Artois. Three kilometres behind these trenches was another German defence position, the Canal-du-Nord.

The plan to capture the Drocourt-Queant line was for the 1st and 4th Canadian Divisions to launch a frontal attack from Dury to Cagnicourt and breach the D-Q line and then advance to the Canal-du-Nord. To accomplish this goal they would have to improve their jump-off positions, and get at least to within 600 metres of the D-Q line. The fighting at Upton Wood continued through the 31st August and 1st September 1918. The Germans would not concede their losses. They heavily counter-attacked Upton Wood but after a few gains, were driven out. The counter-attacks were hurting the Canadians in that they could not properly prepare for the D-Q assault when their own lines were threatened.

From Upton Wood you can see to the south-east, across the D956, an odd shaped wood on an oval shaped hill. This is the Crow's Nest. On 31st August, this important position was still in German hands. It would have to be captured before the D-Q

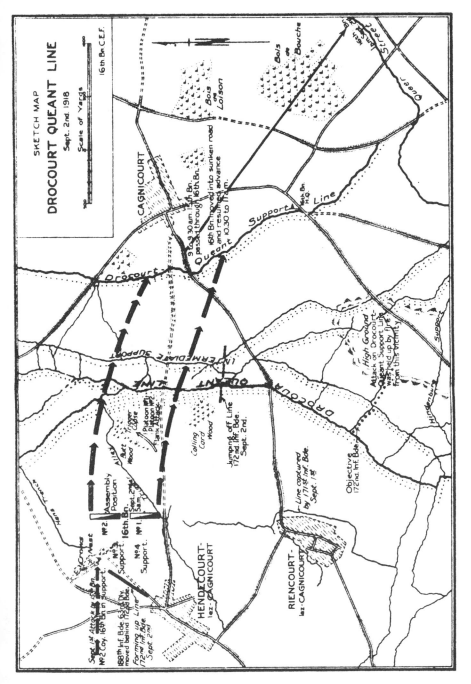

The Attack of the 16th Battalion, September 2, 1918

assault would take place. The objective was given to the 15th Battalion (48th Highlanders of Toronto). They were to capture and hold the Crow's Nest position prior to the main attack on the D-Q line. At 4:50 a.m. the 15th launched their attack and against heavy opposition captured the position and pushed east of the wood. The Germans counter-attacked and with support from the 16th (Western Canadian Scottish) Battalion, the 15th drove the Germans back.

As you look at the Crow's Nest you can see where the Germans had fortified the position. It is now private land so before entering the wood permission should be obtained. This is particularly important in hunting season. The same is true of Upton Wood. The scars of the Great War are evident throughout the wood; enormous shell craters and trenches are still evident. Considering the Wood was only fought over for a few days in 1918 it is amazing the destruction is still evident after 80 years.

Return to your car and continue on the D956 to Dury. After 2 kms a small road to Cagincourt appears on your right. Turn right towards the village. After 1 km the sign for Dominion Cemetery appears. Follow the road to the Cemetery and stop at Dominion Cemetery.

Point 6: The Drocourt-Queant line - Dominion Cemetery

Looking over the open fields in front of you it is hard to imagine what it was like in 1918. Running from Dury village (to your north) through where you stand ran one of the most formidable German trench systems ever constructed. Protected by 4 and 5 belts of barbed wire (each 60 metres wide), with numerous machine-gun posts set-up within the wire the Canadian Corps faced the most difficult task of their illustrious history.

The plan for the attack was simple. The 4th Division was to attack the D-Q line from Dury, to 500 metres south of the Arras-Cambrai Road. The 1st Canadian Division was to attack to the south of the 4th Division to the village of Cagnicourt, and pass through the village, through the woods east of it and capture the Buissy Switch trench system running in front of the Canal-du-Nord.

View of the Crow's Nest from Upton Wood Cemetery.
(PHOTO: N. CHRISTIE)

But the fighting near Haucourt was still raging. The 4th Canadian Division relieved the exhausted 3rd Canadian Division and 11th Imperial Division without their jump-off positions for the D-Q line being secure. This was also true of the Battalions of the 4th Division who relieved units of the 1st Division just south of the Arras-Cambrai Road (D939).

Looking west you can see Upton Wood, The Crows Nest and the village of Hendecourt-les-Cagincourt. It was from these locations the 1st Canadian Division attacked on 2nd September 1918. Due south of where you stand the 16th (Western Canadian Scottish) attacked the D-Q line. The barbed wire held them up and it was due to the courage of Private W. H. Metcalf[3], who in the face of heavy machine-gun fire, ran across the exposed battlefield and using his signal flags got the attention of a tank. He directed the

---

[3] William Henry Metcalf; born Maine, U.S.A., January 19, 1885; died Lewiston, Maine, U.S.A., August 8, 1968.

The 16th Battalion at the Drocourt-Queant line, September 2nd, 1918.

The narrative of Sergeant F.E. Earwaker of Number 4 Platoon, Number 1 Company:

"There were about twenty men between me and the extreme right," Earwaker writes. "I was in a shell-hole with Lance-Corporal Bob Currie of my platoon, two or three privates whose names I have forgotten, and Sergeant Sandy Reid of another company. You couldn't see very clearly. Daylight hadn't quite come.

"We had been there but a short time when Lieut. Campbell-Johnson passed word along to try once more. We all got up together and didn't get more than five yards before we met with the heaviest fire from the trench in front of us that I have ever faced. Down I went into a shell-hole; Lieut. Campbell-Johnson flopped on his stomach right in the wire about twelve feet to my right. Sergeant Reid was about the same distance ahead of me in the wire. Lieut. Campbell-Johnson raised himself on his hands, looking to the front, evidently trying to see how much chance he would have to go forward, when they got him in the head. I then threw out a smoke bomb and Sergeant Reid came back into the shell-hole.

"There we were. Every time we exposed ourselves they opened fire on us from the trench in front, and enfilade fire from the high ground to our right. We decided before making another move to wait for a tank, and soon we heard one to the left about a hundred yards behind us. We signalled to it with our helmets, but the tank did not see us so we sat down to wait, shooting rifle grenades over at the German trench.

"Suddenly a heavy fire started from the trench in front of us. We looked up to see what it was about and there we saw the tank with Lance-Corporal Metcalf walking beside it, a little to the right in front of it, pointing with his signal flags in our direction. It was still pretty early and you could hardly recognize him except by his flags. The tank was coming on at an angle from

Lt. Col. Cy Peck, V.C. and L. Cpl. William Metcalf, V.C. of the 16th (Canadian Scottish) Battalion.

the left flank. I saw Metcalf walking about thirty yards and then we decided it was our turn to help. We made a dash for the trench and made it before the Germans got their guns on us. When we captured the trench, we found a nest of machine guns on not more than a fifty-foot frontage. Behind them was a big dug-out. The tank started to amble out in front the minute we got into the trench; about fifteen minutes later I saw it in smoke five hundred yards in front.

"When the tank came to within three hundred feet of the German wire," writes Private J.H. Riehl, another witness of Metcalf's exploit, "a heavy machine-gun fire was opened upon it from the front trench. Corporal Metcalf jumped up from the shell-hole where he was with his flags pointing towards the enemy's trench, led the tank towards it and then along it. The enemy kept heavy machine-gun fire on the tank and as it got close to the trench commenced to throw at it clusters of bombs tied together.

"When we afterwards got into the trench, we found seventeen German machine-guns at the same place, and all of them had been well used. How Metcalfe escaped being shot to pieces has always been a wonder to me."

tank to the attack. All the while knowing his death would be imminent. Amazingly he survived and was awarded the Victoria Cross. The 16th passed through the front D-Q trench and was again held up by heavy fire. Again the situation was saved by the gallantry of an individual. Lt. Col. Cyrus Peck[4], in the face of harrowing fire, calmly led his men forward with his trusty piper playing them on. For his bravery, Cy Peck was awarded the Victoria Cross. The 16th won 4 Victoria Crosses in the Great War, more than any other individual battalion. The first two were posthumous.

It was after this point the attack flowed smoothly. The 16th attacked and captured Cagnicourt and for the first time it appeared the Germans morale had cracked. Large numbers of Germans surrendered and the Canadians passed through the woods east of Cagnicourt; the Bois de Loison and Bois de Bouche.

The village north-east of you is Villers-les-Cagincourt. It was built into the Buissy Switch. The capture of the front lines and village was the responsibility of the 7th (British Columbia) and the 10th (Alberta) Battalions. The 7th successfully broke throught the front lines and then encountered problems from heavy German fire from their left flank because the 4th Division had encountered severe difficulties (Point 7) on Mont Dury and had not advanced. Private William Rayfield[5] of the 7th Battalion charged ahead of his company attacking a German trench, killing 2 Germans and capturing 10. Later he personally stalked a deadly German sniper and killed him, capturing the trench he was in and 30 of his comrades. Rayfield, not suprisingly, was awarded the Victoria Cross.

The 10th (Alberta) attack met heavy opposition but pushed forward and into the Buissy Switch. Serjeant Arthur Knight[6] single-handedly attacked the German trench in front of Villers-les-Cagnicourt, Knight knocked out one machine-gun and then advanced along the parapet and killed or captured its surprised defenders. He was wounded shortly after and died of his wounds. He is buried in Dominion Cemetery, Plot I, Row F, Grave 15. His actions kept the attack of the 10th Battalion going. He

---

[4] Cyrus Wesley Peck; born Hopewell Hill, New Brunswick, April 26, 1871; died Vancouver, British Columbia, September 27, 1956.
[5] Walter Leigh Rayfield; born Richmond, U.K., October 7, 1881; died Toronto, Ontario, February 19, 1949.
[6] Arthur George Knight; born Haywards Heath, U.K., June 26, 1886; died Viller-les-Cagnicourt, September 3, 1918.

was awarded the Victoria Cross for his bravery. Knight's attack took place roughly 2.5 km east towards Villers-les-Cagnicourt.

The 1st Division's attack had succeeded in cracking the D-Q line. Their advance had slowed but reached the Buissy Switch. To the north things had not gone so well.

Return to your car and return to the D956 to Dury. Turn right and go to the Arras-Cambrai road (D939). Turn right towards Cambrai. After 500 metres turn left at the Canadian Battlefield Park; park in front of the Park and enter the Memorial.

Point 7: Dury Canadian Battlefield Park

This park and memorial commemorates the Canadian Battle of Arras 1918 and the capture of the Drocourt-Queant line. It sits at the southern end of Mont Dury and was part of the Drocourt-Queant support line. The position of the park is excellent for viewing the attack on the Drocourt-Queant line. It is quite over-grown so to get a good view you must walk through the park to it's western boundary.

From here you can see Vis-en-Artois, the water tower at Haucourt, and St. Servins Farm (a few hundred metres east of Haucourt). It was from Haucourt that the 4th Division commenced their attack on the Drocourt-Queant line. The fighting for the Fresnes-Rouvroy line had continued since the end of August and German counterattacks had regained a few of the outlying positions so that immediately prior to the attack on the Drocourt-Queant line the 4th Division had to recapture its own jumping-off positions!

On the night of 1/2 September 1918 the Germans had attacked the jump-off positions of the 38th Battalion (Ottawa). Private Claude Patrick Joseph Nunney[7], DCM, MM, raced through the barrage to his front lines and effectively assisted his comrades in repelling the attack. He continued his fearless actions and was wounded 2nd September and died 16 days later. He is buried in Aubigny Communal Cemetery, west of Arras. He was also awarded the Victoria Cross for his courageous action that day. Nunney was a character of the Canadian Expeditionary Force. His bravery was

---

[7] Claude Patrick Joseph Nunney; born Hastings, U.K., September 24, 1892; died Aubigny, France, September 18, 1918.

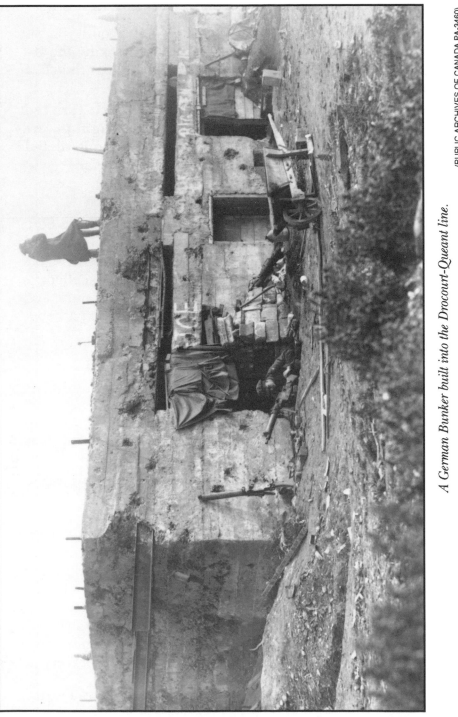

(PUBLIC ARCHIVES OF CANADA PA-3460)

A German Bunker built into the Drocourt-Queant line.

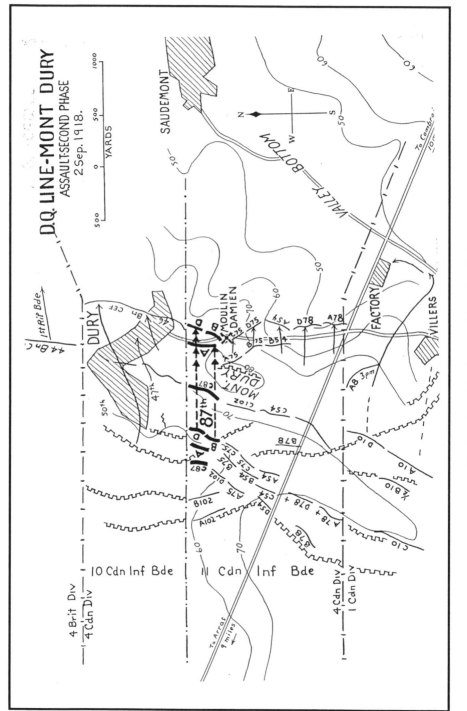

The Attack on Mont Dury, September 2, 1918

(CANADIAN GRENADIER GUARDS)

unchallenged but his discipline not existant. This courageous man had been broken in the ranks 3 times for various insubordinations.

Although the fighting continued, by 5 a.m. the 4th Division was ready to attack from the valley before you and capture Dury. The leading Battalions from north to south were the 50th (Alberta) and the 47th (Western Ontario). They attacked towards Dury village. The 85th (Nova Scotia Highlanders), and 38th (Ottawa) attacked from the St. Servins Farm area. The 72nd (Seaforth Highlanders) attacked just south of the Arras-Cambrai road (directly towards Mont Dury, where you are standing).

They crossed the valley and advanced through barbed wire and into the German front line and up the rise to the D-Q Support line (passing through the Canadian Park). They continued to the crest of Mont Dury. When the attack crossed the crest they were hit by a withering fire from Dury, Villers-les-Cagnicourt and from a sunken road running south-east from Dury to Villers. The 4th Division attack was stopped in its tracks.

Walk to the northern boundary of the Park. From this vantage point the attack of the 50th and 47th battalions towards Dury village can be observed.The 46th (South Saskatchewan) passed through the 50th and entered the village. They fought for the village and later supported by the 44th (Manitoba) captured most of it. They were unable to proceed much past the eastern edge of the village due to the machine-gun fire from the sunken road and other German positions. Advancing was impossible. It was also at this time that further disaster hit the 4th Division. The supporting battalions, the 75th (Mississauga Horse), 102nd (Central Ontario) and 87th (Grenadier Guards of Montreal), planning on passing through to further attack towards the east, advanced prematurely and caught up to the attacking troops. Caught with so many men in the open ground the troops were easy targets for the German fire.

Two Victoria Crosses were awarded for bravery in aiding the exposed Canadian wounded on Mont Dury. Private John Francis Young[8] of the 87th and Captain B.S. Hutcheson[9], a medical officer

---

[8] John Francis Young; born Kidderminster, U.k., January 14, 1893; died Montreal, November 7, 1929.

[9] Bellenden Seymour Hutcheson; born Mount Carmel, USA, December 16, 1893; died Cairo, Illinois, April 9, 1954.

The Dury Canadian Memorial

(PHOTO: N. CHRISTIE)

THE DURY CANADIAN MEMORIAL

The Canadian monument at Dury, east of the City of Arras, stands on one of eight First World War Canadianbattlefields officially commemorated.

In 1920, the Canadian Battlefield Monument Commission decided to erect memorials at:

St. Julien - to commemorate the Second Battle of Ypres

Hill 62 - to commemorate the Battle of Mount Sorrel

Courcelette - to commemorate the Battle of the Somme

Vimy - to commemorate the Battle of Vimy Ridge

Passchendaele - to commemorate the Battle of Passchendaele

Le Quesnel - to commemorate the Battle of Amiens

Dury - to commemorate the Battle of Arras 1918 and the capture of the Drocourt-Queant line

Bourlon Wood - to commemorate the Battles of the Canal du Nord, Cambrai, the capture of Valenciennes and Mons and the March to the Rhine

It was decided that Vimy would act as the National Memorial and have a unique design. The other seven wouldbe marked with identical memorials. A competition was held to choose an architect to design the monuments. Walter Allward of Toronto was chosen for Vimy's unique memorial and Frederick C. Clemesha of Regina took second place. Clemesha's design, "The Brooding Soldier," was built at St. Julien and had such a stark effect at its unveiling in 1923 that the Monument Commission decided it also should remain unique.

In conjunction with the architectural advisor, P. E. Nobbs, the cube design was developed for the remaining six monuments. A 13-tonne block of Stanstead granite was used for each. A wreath was carved into two sides of the monument and on the other two sides was engraved a brief explanation of the exploits of the Canadian Corps in that specific battle. One side is in English, the other in French.

At Dury, the monument reads:

THE CANADIAN CORPS 100,000 STRONG ATTACKED AT ARRAS ON AUGUST 26TH 1918. STORMED SUCCESSIVE GERMAN LINES AND HERE ON SEPT. 2ND BROKE AND TURNED THE MAIN GERMAN POSITION ON THE WESTERN FRONT AND REACHED THE CANAL DU NORD.

Around the base of the stone, it reads:

HONOUR TO CANADIANS WHO ON THE FIELDS OF FLANDERS AND OF FRANCE FOUGHT IN THE CAUSE OF THE ALLIES WITH SACRIFICE AND DEVOTION

As with all of the Canadian Memorials on the Western Front, these words hardly capture the spirit of sacrifice and devotion of the men of the Canadian Corps in the Battle of Arras 1918. It was a magnificent victory which cost more than 5,000 Canadian men their lives.

attached to the 75th Battalion, continuously dressed wounded under extremely heavy fire and somehow managed to survive.

By nightfall the Canadian position was precarious, the troops exhausted. But, unkown to them, the Battle of the Wills had been won. Although the action continued on the 3rd September, and Canadian units continued to push east the Germans had admitted defeat and were planning a withdrawal behind the Canal-du-Nord, 4 km east of Dury.

The pressure exerted on the Germans had cost the Canadians 11,000 dead and wounded, but it had ultimately been too much for the Germans. The Germans had been defeated and lost a defensive system they knew was impregnable. It shattered their defensive strategy and it was the Canadian Corps who had delivered the Coup de Grace.

Return to the front of the park. From this position to the west you can see Vis-en-Artois village, Upton Wood, The Crow's Nest, Cagnicourt village and, with binoculars, Dominion Cemetery (a small group of trees in the open fields north of Cagnicourt village). While the battle was raging on Mont Dury, the 1st Division was storming across the fields south of you.

The Buissy Switch joined with the main Drocourt-Queant line just west of Mont Dury and ran south-east across the Arras-Cambrai road 100 metres west of you; then south-east in front of the village of Buissy, then due south to Inchy-en-Artois where it met the Hindenburg line. The 72nd (Seaforth Highlanders of Vancouver), 7th (British Columbia) and the 10th (Alberta) had attacked the Buissy Switch at Villers-les-Cagnicourt (the village visible 1.5 km south-east of you) and pierced the line. It was this success that ultimately made the German position untenable.

Return to your car and continue towards Cambrai after 1 km turn left for Dury village. This sunken road was the thorn in the side of the 4th Division on Mont Dury. It was heavily defended and although some of it was captured on the 2nd September 1918. The Germans counterattacked and regained the positions. The value of the D-Q line to the Germans was evident by the quantity and quality of German reinforcements pumped into the battle. Drive into the village turning left and left again at the church and left again to go to Dury Crucifix Cemetery. Stop at the cemetery.

The ruins of the Windmill on Mont Dury.
(PUBLIC ARCHIVES OF CANADA PA-4397)

View of Dury Village, accross Mont Dury, from Dury Mill Cemetery.

Point 8: Dury Crucifix Cemetery

From this point looking south you can see Mont Dury, the crest where Battalions of the 4th Division were cut to ribbons. The village of Dury was captured by the 46th (Saskatchewan) on the 2nd September 1918. Many members of the 46th are buried in Plot I of Dury Crucifix Cemetery. The village itself was the scene of heavy fighting and by the end of the day the Canadian line was at its eastern edge. The fighting north of the Arras-Cambrai road inflicted heavy casualties on the 4th Division, and for a large part unnecessary, casualties. The 102nd Battalion used only one company in the battle and suffered 186 casualties. On 3/4 September 1918 units of the 4th Division pushed northeast and east of Dury Village towards Recourt and Rumancourt. The Germans had decided their positions west of the Canal-du-Nord were untenable. Although they still held on, another successful attack could leave German forces west of the Canal cut-off. They decided to withdraw.

Return to your car and drive back to the Arras/Cambrai road, continue straight across the D939 and drive into the village of Villers-les-Cagnicourt. The Buissy Switch ran just west of the village and provided a major secondary defense for the Germans. The village was cleared by the 10th (Alberta) Battalion on the second. It was at Villers that Sergeant Arthur George Knight won his Victoria Cross (see Point 6). Turn left at the 'T' junction and drive into the village. At the eastern edge of town turn right on the 'T' junction on the D13 to Cagnicourt. Follow the road into Cagnicourt. It was at Cagnicourt the Canadians saw the first indications of the collapse of German morale when a whole German battalion surrendered. The Drocourt-Queant Support line ran in a south-east direction just west of the village. In the centre of the village at the 'T' junction turn right on the D14E to Inchy-en-Artois, follow the signs to Queant Road Cemetery, 2 kilometres down the D14E. Turn left on the D14 at the village cemetery towards Buissy, after 1.5 kms stop.

Point 9: Buissy Switch

Looking west, the first large wood on the right is the Bois de Bouche, on it's right is the Bois de Loison, and north of the Bois

War Diary of the 50th Battalion, Alberta Regiment, Septmber 2nd, 1918.

Weather Fine - Wind South West - Ground dry.

ZERO hour at 5. A.M. and promptly on the second every gun for miles on either side opened fire and furnished the heaviest and most effective barrage ever experienced by our troops. Our leading waves were immediately on top of the Machine Gun posts which had given the Seaforths so much trouble, and disposed of them in quick order, the suddenness of the attack and the terrific bombardment evidently taking them by surprise. The troops covered the 500 yards to the enemy front line in quick time and found it necessary to wait until the barrage lifted to enable them to charge the first trench. When the barrage lifted our men were into the trench and at work with bayonet and bombs and only a minute or so elapsed before every Hun was accounted for, hundreds of that surrendered and were sent back to Battalion Headquarters together with their wounded and any of our own casualties.

Some of their Machine Gun crews fought well but all those found in the dugouts showed a willingness to surrender.

The succeeding waves experienced a repetition of these conditions in the remaining trenches and promptly to the minute of the last barrage line lifting from the limit of the area allotted to this Battalion their task was completed and the DROCOURT-QUEANT LINE captured with every dug-out tunnel thoroughly mopped up.

Foremost among the brilliant work done during the attack was that of Lieut. A.J. SLADE, O.C. "D" Company.

During the action his Company alone took over four hundred prisoners and dozens of Machine Guns. This was due in a great extent to the untiring efforts of Lieut. SLADE who seemed to be everywhere at once, encouraging and directing his men and urging them on to even greater efforts. Twice he personally charged and captured Machine Gun Posts, once with a handful of men to assist, the second, with only his batman.

Captain A.R. BATSON, M.C. displayed his usual high qualities of leadership in capturing his objectives and again and again undoubtedly saved a large number of casualties through his masterful tactics in disposing of enemy Machine Gun Positions. After his position had been consolidated and his men protected as fas as possible against enemy shell fire, he was killed while discussing the situation with the Company Commander on his flank.

The Battalion loses in Capt. A.R. BATSON, M.C., one of the oldest and most trusted Company Commanders it has ever possessed.

Captain S.A. MOORE, M.C. O.C. "A" Company also met his death by the same shell that killed Capt. Batson, after also leading his Company successfully through the most brilliant attack ever made by the Battalion.

Captain MOORE represented the dashing style of Company Commander, yet was always mindful of the welfare of his men. No situation was too difficult for him to tackle and win.

Every Officer, N.C.O. and man in the Battalion lived up to the high standard that has carried the Unit so successfully through VIMY, the SOMME, PASSCHENDAELE, AMIENS and other battles.

Major J.LR. PARRY did invaluable work in reconnaissance of the situation before and after the attack.

Lieut. A.M. AITKEN, Lieut. W.H. KIRCHNER D.L.M., Lieut. P.W. BROWN, Lieut. J.R. HARRIS, Lieut. S.G. MCCONNELL and Lieut. R. GORDON displayed brilliant qualities of leadership and their examples were of inestimable value to all ranks.

No. 434218, Sgt. J.H. DOWLER, Signalling Sergeant, displayed wonderful gallantry in his efforts to maintain communication between Companies and Headquarters and was the first to inform Battn. Headquarters that the Companies had attained their objectives. He personally sent back situation reports on several occasions that were of the utmost value.

No. 696187, Sgt. R.M. TUFTS, M.M. tackled a Machine Gun Post alone, bayonetting eight of the enemy enabling his Platoon to advance after being held up by fire from this point.

No. 808871, Pte. Chas DAVIS, after being severely injured by a kick from a horse precious to the operation carried on and besides other brilliant exploits he personally tackled an enemy strong point unaided, bombing and killing several of the enemy and capturing fifty prisoner.

The foregoing are only a few of the many instances of exceptional valor displayed by men of all ranks in the Battle.

Our casualties were extremely light during the attack, but shortly afterwards a heavy barrage was laid down on our newly captured position, which unfortunately caught a large number. His fire, however, died down towards evening and was then principally confined to gas shelling. Battalion Headquarters moved forward to the Chalk Pit at DURY early in the forenoon and the Battalion was disposed in the two trenches of the DROCOURT-QUEANT Line, immediately west of DURY. Battalion on our left having been unable to proceed.

Over 1000 Prisoners were captured, besides 90 Machine Guns, two anti-tank Guns, two Minnenwerfer Machines and other war material.

Nine different Regiments were identified, prisoners from sixteen Battalions of these Regiments having been brought in. The Area Commandant of DURY was also captured together with five Medical Officers.

| Casualties- | 2 Killed in Action - | 2 Officers Wounded |
| | 29 O.R's Killed in Action- | 181 OR's Wounded |

is the Village of Villers-Les-Cagincourt. The village north-east is Buissy/Baralle, 1 kilometre west of the Canal-du-Nord. The village south-south-east is Inchy-en-Artois which is on the Canal-du-Nord and was an important jump-off point for the Canadians in the assault on the Canal-du-Nord, September 27th, 1918. The main fortification between the Canadians and the Canal was the Buissy Switch which ran from Villers-Les-Cagincourt to Buissy and then south to Inchy. At Inchy the Buissy Switch connected to the main Hindenburg Line and ran due south. From your position, looking towards Villers-les-Cagnicourt you can see where the 10th (Alberta) cracked the Buissy Switch and established their presence so close to the Canal-du-Nord on the night of 2nd September 1918.

Look north-west towards the two woods, the Bois de Loison and the Bois de Bouche. This was the area quickly captured on the 2nd by the 14th (Royal Montreal Regiment) and the 15th (48th Highlanders of Toronto) battalions. The units advanced towards the Buissy Switch and actually entered the German line, right at the point where you are standing.

Further south the British units had been unable to keep up with the Canadian advance, and the right flanking Canadian Battalions were unable to penetrate the Switch. However, the pressure had been sufficient, even if a complete breakthrough was not achieved, to convince the Germans their defenses west of the Canal were lost.

The final battle of the war for the Canadians would take place 3 weeks later, when again the Canadian Corps would be chosen to attack the major German defensive positions defending Cambrai.

Return to your car and drive towards Buissy through Baralle, turn left on the D14 and rejoin the D939. Turn left on the D939 towards Arras. Follow the D939 until you reach Vis-en-Artois, turn right on the D9E towards Boiry-Notre Dame. After 2.5 kilometres you reach the village of Boiry-Notre Dame. Turn left on the D34 to Monchy-le-Preux. 500 metres outside of Boiry, stop. We are returning to the battlefield of August 26th-28th, 1918. This is the area captured by the 3rd Division.

Point 10: The Fresnes-Rouvroy Line - Boiry-Notre-Dame
The main German fortification line, the Fresnes-Rouvroy line ran

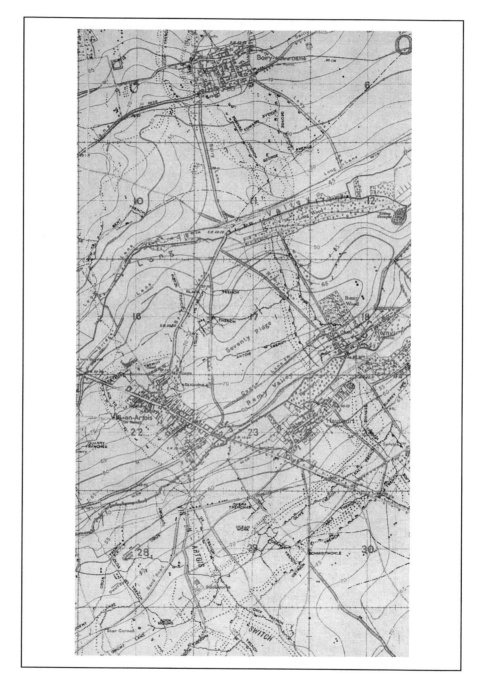

Trench map showing the Fresnes rouvroy Line from Boiry to Haucourt

in a north-south direction from the Scarpe River, just east of Jigsaw Wood, through the western outskirts of Boiry-Notre-Dame (100 metres east of you), then south-east towards the villages of Remy and Haucourt, with a loop encompassing the village of Vis-en-Artois.

On the 28th August the 58th (Central Ontario) Battalion attacked the Fresnes-Rouvroy line from this position and with the 52nd (Northern Ontario), broke through the line, swept through the village and established posts to the east of Boiry. This attack by the 58th was tremendously successful and by cracking the northern flank, endangered the whole German line.

A major stategy of the German defense was the use of Machine Gun Battalions. They added an enormous capacity of machine-gun fire that could crack any Canadian attack. The Canadians responded with a quick change of policy. The 58th Battalion employed snipers with each attacking platoon specifically to pick-off the German machine-gunners. Looking west to Monchy you will see a large wood roughly 200 metres west. This is the Bois du

Vert. It was captured by the 52nd (New Ontario) Battalion on the 27th August 1918. North of the Bois du Vert you can see where 58th (Central Ontario) attacked at Bois du Sart (no longer there) and due north roughly 800 metres you can see the approximate location of Jigsaw Wood where the 42nd (Black Watch of Montreal) and the Princess Patricia's Canadian Light Infantry successfully attacked on the 27-28 August 1918.

Before you rejoin your car look southwards to Vis-en-Artois and south-east to Haucourt and Remy. On the 28th August the 4-C.M.R and the 43rd (Cameron Highlanders of Winnipeg) Battalions attacked and captured Remy, Haucourt and Vis-en-Artois.

Continue on the D34 for 2 kms, turn right and follow the road into Monchy-le-Preux. Monchy was the scene of heavy fighting in the First Battle of Arras in 1917. It was captured on 11th April, 1917. When you meet the town square you will see the Monchy Newfoundland Memorial (it is worth a stop). Go left through the village and follow the signs to Monchy British Cemetery (Chemin d'Arras). Follow the Chemin d'Arras over the Motorway into an industrial estate. You are driving over the area captured by the Canadian Mounted Rifles on 26th August, 1918. Just south of the village was the scene of Lieutenant Charles Rutherford's[10] (of the 5th CMR) dazzling exploits: He single-handedly captured several machine-guns and helped drive the advance forward. He was awarded the Victoria Cross.

Continue until the road meets a 'T' junction with the D37 to Feuchy. Turn right and follow the road 1.5 kilometres and turn right at the Orange Hill Cemetery signpost. Drive to the cemetery. Stop and enter the cemetery.

Point 11: Orange Hill

Looking north from the Cemetery you can see the village of Feuchy in the Scarpe River Valley. The Scarpe River runs east-west from Arras. You can see from left to right, Arras, St. Laurent-Blangy, Athies, Feuchy, Fampoux, Roeux. This area was the scene of heavy fighting in April-May 1917. North of the Scarpe River

---

[10] Caherles Smith Rutherford; born Haldimand Township, Ontario. January 9, 1892.

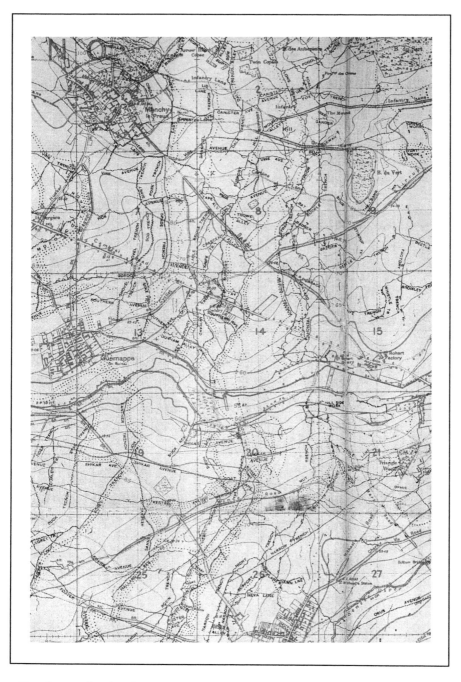

Trench map showing German trench systems, east and south of Monchy-le-Preux.

Monchy-le-Preux German Observation Post at the highest point.
(PUBLIC ARCHIVES OF CANADA PA-4437)

you can see the 9th Highland Division Cairn Memorial erected on the Point-du-Jour. Well to the north-west you can also see (on a clear day) Vimy Ridge and further west the French National Memorial on Notre-Dame du Lorette Ridge.

For the Battle of 1918, the 3rd Canadian Division attacked from a line 500 metres east of Feuchy village, due south past the western slope of Orange Hill (100 metres east of where you now stand), to the Arras-Cambrai Road. The objectives of the three assaulting battalions, from north to south, 4th Canadian Mounted Rifles (Toronto) were to attack between Feuchy and Orange Hill, The 2nd CMR (Central Ontario) attacked up Orange Hill (where you now stand) and the 5th CMR (Eastern Townships), attacked directly through the German lines to capture Monchy-le-Preux. The 1st CMR (Saskatchewan) passed through the 2nd CMR on Orange Hill and attacked north of Monchy. From Orange Hill Cemetery the church steeple of Monchy can be seen just over the Hill to the east. You can also see Pelves, the village (on the south side of the Scarpe) 3 1/2 kms east of where you stand. Pelves and the territory from where you stand were the objectives of the sec-

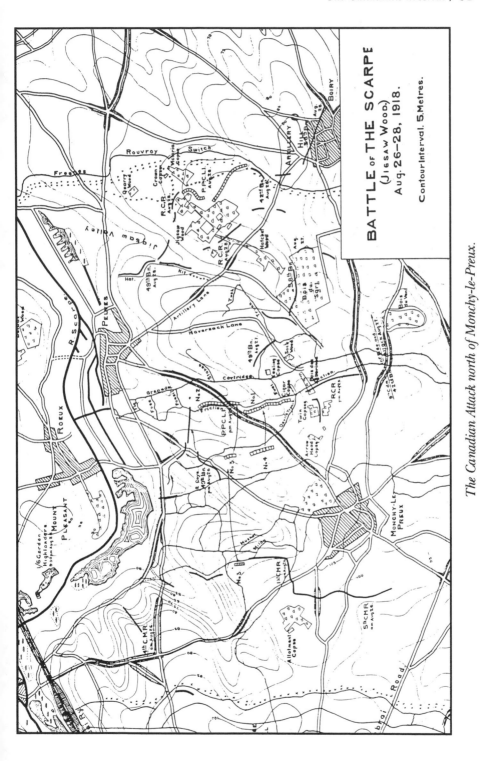

The Canadian Attack north of Monchy-le-Preux.

ond phase of the 3rd Division attack. The 49th (Edmonton Regiment) and Princess Patricia's Canadian Light Infantry attacked on the 26th-28th August 1918 with the 49th capturing Pelves on the 28th. To achieve these gains the 3rd Division had to break through three German defensive lines and protect their left flank from enfilade fire from the north side on the Scarpe River. The 51st Highland Division supported the Canadian attack north of the Scarpe and kept up a protective flank. Throughout the Battle the 51st successfully advanced alongside the Canadians. The battlefields both north and south of the Scarpe River had been fought over unsuccessfully in April-May 1917 with very heavy losses. In 1918, gains beyond the dreams of the other major attacks launched in 1917, were captured by the Canadian Corps in 3 days!

Return to your car proceed to the Feuchy road, turn left and return to the Arras-Cambrai Road. Turn right and return to Arras. In the left distance a ridge cuts across the Arras-Cambrai road. This is Chapel Hill and Feuchy Chapel Cemetery is on the right, 200 metres, west of Chapel Hill. Outside of Tilloy a wood is passed on your left, it was the Canadian jump-off line for 26 August, 1918.

CEMETERIES AND MEMORIALS OF THE BATTLE OF ARRAS AND THE DROCOURT-QUEANT LINE
August - September 1918

The Battles of the Canadian Corps in 1918 were enormously successful by First World War standards. Consequently the men who died received known and honoured burial from their comrades. Of the men killed in battles that were less successful, like the Battle of Ypres 1915, the Somme 1916 or Passchendaele 1917, only a small percentage have known graves. For the Battle of Arras 1918 more than 90% of the men killed or died as a result of wounds have a known grave.

The cemeteries are usually small and lie in the farmers' fields off the Arras-Cambrai road. Many are just as the Canadian Corps Burial Officer left them in 1918. They preserve in perpetuity the famous actions of 1918.

Sadly these cemeteries are a little out of the way and are rarely visited. Somehow, they seem forgotten. It is a tragedy that the sacrifices of the volunteers and conscripts of 1918 have become so irrelevant.

The list below outlines the major cemeteries where the men who died breaking the Hindenburg line lie buried. Those with no known grave, are commemorated by name only on the Vimy Memorial, 8 kms north of Arras (all 11,285 Canadians killed in France that have no known grave are commemorated at Vimy). The 6895 Canadian soldiers with no known grave and who died in Belgium are commemorated on the Menin Gate Memorial to the Missing at Ypres (Ieper), Belgium). Only 300-400 of the 11,000 names engraved around the base of the memorial are soldiers killed at Arras 1918 or at the Drocourt-Queant line.

Several of these cemeteries will appear unusual in their make-up, in that they contain a high percentage of unknowns. The reason for this lies with disastrous British attacks in the Battle of Arras, 1917. Thousands of British soldiers were killed in these futile attacks and their bodies remained on the battlefields and were only covered with a few feet of earth for hygiene reasons.

The view from Wancourt British Cemetery, Monchy-le-Preux on the mid-horizon

(PHOTO: N. CHRISTIE)

During the Battlefield clearances, 1919-21, thousands of these remains were concentrated into the small cemeteries originally made by the Canadians in 1918. The cemeteries used for these concentrations were, principally, Tilloy, Wancourt, Feuchy Chapel, Dury, Crucifix, and Vis-en-Artois.

TILLOY BRITISH CEMETERY, Tilloy-les-Mofflaines

The cemetery is located on the SE side of the village, which is 3 kms south-east of Arras just south of the Arras- Cambrai road.

The cemetery was originally made in 1917 and used by the Canadians (Plot II) in 1918. The cemetery was enlarged by battlefield clearances after the war and now contains the graves of 1,627 Commonwealth soldiers. 57 are Canadian of which 6 are unidentified. The majority are men of the 2nd Canadian Infantry Division.

Michael Bernard McCool
Private
46th (Saskatchewan) Battalion
Died of wounds September 3, 1918.
Born in Londonderry, Ireland, in May
1894. Son of Mary and William
McCool of Derry, Ireland. Came to
Canada in 1913.
Enlisted in March 1916, and served
in France from 1917. He was severely
wounded in 1917 but recovered and
returned to France.
At Dury, on September 2nd, 1918 he
was wounded in the chest by shrapnel
from an enemy shell. His wound was
dressed and he was taken the
Regimental Aid Post and later
evacuated to No. 33 Casualty
Clearing Station, where he died.

William Broder McTaggart
Major
Canadian Field Artillery
Killed in action September 2, 1918.
Born at Clinton, Ontario, April 19th,
1893. He was the son of George and
Nettie McTaggart of Cinton.
Appointed Lieutenant August 1914.
Promoted to Major and awarded the
Distinguished Service Order in 1918.
He commanded the 12th Battery,
Canadian Field Artillery in France.
On September 2nd, 1918 while at the
Observation Post at Dury, directing
the fire of his battery he was hit and
instantly killed by enemy machine
gun fire. His body was brought back
to Arras and Buried in Faubourg-
D'Amiens Cemetery. He had been
wounded 4 times.

TIGRIS LANE CEMETERY, Wancourt

The cemetery is located on the Tilloy-Wancourt road, 2 kms east of Tilloy British Cemetery. The cemetery was made in 1917 and used by the Canadians in 1918.

It contains the graves of 119 Commonwealth soldiers of which 33 are Canadian (1 is unidentified). The majority are men of the 2nd Canadian Division and are buried in Plot II.

FEUCHY CHAPEL BRITISH CEMETERY, Wancourt

The cemetery is located on the Arras-Cambrai road 8 kms SE of Arras.

It was made in 1917 and later used by the Canadians Corps. After the war it was greatly enlarged by battlefield clearances.

It now contains the graves of 1,089 Commonwealth soldiers of which 26 are Canadian (6 are unidentified). They are buried in Plot I.

WANCOURT BRITISH CEMETERY

The cemetery is located east of the village, which is 2 kms south of the main Arras-Cambrai road, 8 kms south-east of Arras.

The cemetery was made in 1917 and used by the Canadian Corps in 1918. It was enlarged by battlefield clearances after the war.

It now contains the graves of 1,839 Commonwealth soldiers of which 246 are Canadian (24 are unidentified). The majority of the Canadians are men of the 2nd Canadian Division killed in the vicinity 27-28 August 1918.

The 72nd Battalion (Seaforth Highlanders of Vancouver) buried 60 of their number who fell in the battle of the Drocourt-Queant line, September 2nd, 1918 in Wancourt. They are predominantly buried in Plots II and III.

Lieutenant Colonel Archibald McKenzie, DSO and bar, Commander of the 26th Battalion (New Brunswick) is buried in plot II Row C grave 9. He was killed in action in the assault on the Fresnes-Rouvroy line, south of Vis-en-Artois, 28 August 1918. He was 39.

Wancourt British Cemetery, circa 1928

ORANGE HILL CEMETERY, Feuchy

The cemetery is located 2 kms south-east of Feuchy village, which is 5 kms east of Arras and 3 kms north of the Arras- Cambrai road.

The cemetery was made by the Canadian Corps Burial Officer in August 1918.

It contains the graves of 42 Canadian soldiers. The Canadians buried here are virtually all 3rd Division killed in the capture of Orange Hill, August 26th, 1918. In row B, 8 members of the 58th Battalion (Central Ontario) killed by a shell near the wagon lines near Feuchy are buried. They had completed three days of heavy and successful fighting near Boiry-Notre Dame and had just been relieved.

Of the 42 burials 8 are those of officers.

WINDMILL BRITISH CEMETERY, Monchy-le-Preux

The cemetery is located on the Arras-Cambrai road at the turn off for Monchy village. It is 8 kms south-east of Arras.

It was made in 1917 and used by the Canadian Corps in August-September 1918.

It contains the graves of 401 Commonwealth soldiers of which 61 are Canadian (2 are unidentified). The majority of the Canadian burials (Plot II) are men of the 2nd Division killed 26-27 August 1918.

MONCHY BRITISH CEMETERY

The cemetery is located 2 kms west of the village, which is 8 kms from Arras.

It was made in 1917 and used by the Canadian Corps in August 1918.

It contains the graves of 552 Commonwealth soldiers of which 23 are Canadian (Plot II, rows C and D). 10 of the burials belong to the Canadian Field Artillery killed in September 1918. The balance are men of the 3rd Canadian Division.

SUN QUARRY CEMETERY, Cherisy

The cemetery is located east of the village on the road to Hendecourt. Cherisy is 15 kms south-east of Arras.

The cemetery was made by the Canadian Corps Burial Officer in September-October 1918.

It contains the graves of 191 Commonwealth soldiers of which 160 are Canadian (7 are unidentified). The men of the 2nd Division particularly the 26th Battalion (New Brunswick) and the 24th Battalion (Queen Victoria's Rifles of Montreal) make-up the majority of the burials. These men were killed 27-28 August 1918 in the capture of Cherisy and the ensuing effort on the Fresnes-Rouvroy line south of Vis-en-Artois.

QUEBEC CEMETERY, Cherisy

The cemetery is located 1 km north of Sun Quarry Cemetery.

It was made by the Canadian Corps Burial Officer in September 1918.

It contains the graves of 195 Commonwealth soldiers of which 189 are Canadian. The burials are largely those of the men of the 2nd Canadian Division killed 28th August 1918 in the failed attack on the Fresnes-Rouvroy line south of Vis- en-Artois. The men of the 22nd Battalion (Canadien-Francais) and the 24th Battalion (Queen Victoria's Rifles of Montreal) represent the majority of the burials. Both Battalions are Quebec Regiments consequently gave the name to the cemetery.

VALLEY CEMETERY, Vis-en-Artois

This beautiful, little cemetery is located 2 km south-west of the village on the road to Cherisy. Vis-en-Artois is 12 kms south-east of Arras on the Arras-Cambrai road.

The cemetery was made by the Canadian Corps in September 1918. It was enlarged by 28 graves in 1924-25.

It now contains the graves of 69 Commonwealth soldiers of which 37 are Canadian. The cemetery is located in the farmers' fields and from it can be seen Quebec Cemetery on the rise to the east. It is one of the most beautiful cemeteries in France. The Canadians buried here are principally 3rd Battalion (Toronto Regiment) killed in the hand-to-hand fighting in Orix Trench, part of the Fresnes-Rouvroy line south of Vis-en-Artois.

Amongst the 37 Canadians buried here 7 were decorated for bravery, of the 7, 3 were decorated twice for bravery. Lieutenant Edward Slattery of the 3rd Battalion was decorated 4 times for bravery. He was awarded the Distinguished Conduct Medal, and the Military Medal 3 times. The DCM was awarded for gallantry at Fresnoy in 1917 and the Military Medals were awarded for bravery at the Somme, September 1916, Vimy Ridge, April 1917 and Passchendaele November 1917. Slattery lived in Point St. Charles in Montreal and was born in Newfoundland. He was 23.

VIS-EN-ARTOIS BRITISH CEMETERY, Haucourt

The cemetery is located in the village of Haucourt just east of Vis-en-Artois on the main Arras-Cambrai road, 12 kms south-east of Arras.

The cemetery was made by the Canadian Corps in September 1918 and enlarged by battlefield clearances after the war which brought in a further 1,901 graves.

It now contains the graves of 2,335 Commonwealth soldiers of which 582 are Canadian (59 are unidentified). It is the largest cemetery which reflects the fighting at Arras and the Drocourt-Queant line in 1918. The original burials in Plot I and II reflect the battles around Vis-en-Artois, August 28th to 31st, and the storming of the D-Q line near Dury September 2nd, 1918. Many headstones bear 2 names indicating a trench burial.

The battlefield clearances brought in many Canadian graves from the battlefields north of Vis-en-Artois such as Boiry-Notre Dame, Remy, Pelves, Jigsaw Woodand the Bois du Sart. These men are mainly of the 3rd Canadian Division. The Princess Patricia's Canadian Light Infantry, Royal Canadian Regiment and the 4th Canadian Mounted Rifle Battalions are particularly in evidence.

At the back of the cemetery is the Vis-en-Artois Memorial to the Missing for the Advance to Victory in France. The Memorial records the names of 9,903 British and South African soldiers, who died between August 8th, 1918 and November 11th, 1918 and have no known grave.

UPTON WOOD CEMETERY, Hendecourt-les-Cagincourt

The cemetery is located beside Upton Wood just off the road leading from Hendecourt to Dury, 2 kms north of the village.

The cemetery was made by the Canadian Corps in September 1918. It contains the graves of 226 Commonwealth soldiers of which 217 are Canadian (8 are unidentified). The burials reflect the actions of the 1st Canadian Division at Upton Wood, the Crow's Nest and the attack on the Drocourt-Queant line,.

DOMINION CEMETERY, Hendecourt-les-Cagincourt

The cemetery is located 2 kms north of the village in an open field, which is 4 kms south of the main Arras-Cambrai road.

The cemetery was made by the Canadian Corps in September 1918.

It contains the graves of 230 Commonwealth soldiers of which 213 are Canadian (3 are unidentified). The cemetery reflects the attack by the 1st Canadian Division on the Drocourt-Queant line, September 2nd, 1918. Buried in plot I, Row C, grave 25 and row G, grave 13 are Lieutenant Alex Campbell-Johnston and Private Ronald Campbell-Johnston both sons of Amy Campbell-Johnston of Vancouver. Alex had enlisted with the 16th Battalion (Western Canadian Scottish) when only 16 in 1915 and had served in France from 1916. He was killed at the D-Q line September 2nd, 1918. He was only 18. Ronald, his 29 year old brother was a private in the 7th Battalion (British Columbia). He was killed at the D-Q line, September 3rd, 1918.

In plot I, row F, grave 15, is buried Sergeant A. G. Knight VC of the 10th Battalion (Alberta). He won his Victoria Cross, posthumously for conspicuous bravery, September 2nd, 1918 in the attack on the D-Q line.

DURY MILL CEMETERY, Dury

The cemetery is located 1 km south of the village which is 3 km north of the Arras-Cambrai road.

The cemetery was made by the Canadian Corps in September 1918.

It now contains the graves of 335 Commonwealth soldiers of which 324 are Canadian (11 are unidentified). The burials represent the difficult attack of the 4th Canadian Division across Mont Dury. The results of having too many men concentrated in an open area is all too evident.

Buried in plot I, row B, graves 17 and 35, are Clifford and Norval Bell of Kincardine, Ontario. Both were killed on the September 2nd, 1918 whilst serving with the 78th Battalion

Dury Crucifix Cemetery, circa 1928.

(Winnipeg Grenadiers). They were 22 and 25 years old respectively.

The view looking of the cemetery gives a clear picture of the terrain over which the Canadians attacked from Vis-en-Artois.

DURY CRUCIFIX CEMETERY, Dury

The cemetery is located on the south side of the village near the Water Tower. The village is located 3 km north of the Arras-Cambrai road.

It was made by the Canadian Corps in September 1918 (Plot I, rows A and B) and was greatly enlarged after the war from battlefield clearances, mostly from the Battle of Arras 1917.

It now contains the graves of 2,058 Commonwealth soldiers of which 1,766 (86%) are unidentified. 162 Canadians are buried here, of which 42 are unidentified. The original burials were men of the 4th Division killed in the capture of Dury (particularly the 46th Battalion (Saskatchewan) September 2nd and 3rd, 1918. The battlefield clearances resulted in 90 Canadian burials from north and west of Dury, being brought here.

These men were largely 4th Division who were killed at Dury. The 50th Battalion (Alberta) and the 44th Battalion (Manitoba) were the main concentrations, however some 3rd Division men killed August 27th-28th were brought into the cemetery.

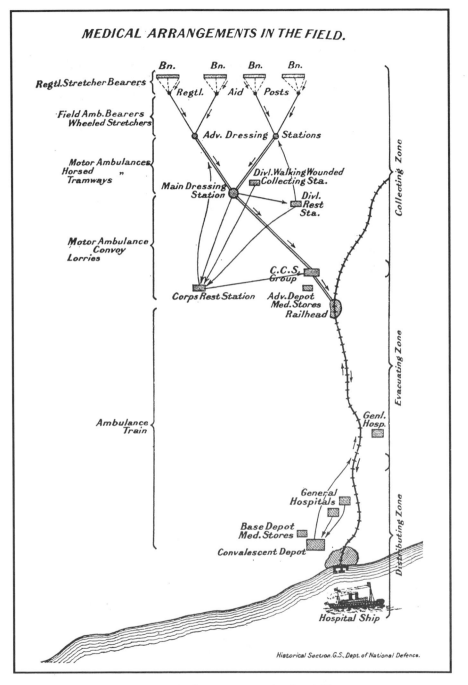

Medical Arrangement in the Field.

Details of the Air Forces Memorial in Faubourg D'Amiens

(PHOTOS: N. CHRISTIE)

QUEANT ROAD CEMETERY, Buissy

The cemetery is located east of the village of Queant which is 3 kms south of the Arras-Cambrai road.

It was made by fighting units in October 1918 and enlarged by the concentration of 2,226 graves from battlefield clearances, in particular from around Bullecourt, the scene of fierce Australian fighting in 1917. Two thirds of the burials are unidentified.

It now contains the graves of 2,323 Commonwealth soldiers, including 87 Canadians (5 are unidentified). Half of the Canadians brought into the cemetery were killed in the attack on the Drocourt-Queant line.

From the cemetery there is an excellent view of the battlefields over which the Canadian Corps attacked, September 2nd, 1918.

In plot VIII, Row C, grave 10, is buried Captain Percy Cherry, VC, MC of the 26th Battalion Australian Imperial Force. His Victoria Cross was awarded posthumously for bravery March 27th, 1917.

The system for the evacuation of the wounded was very efficient by 1918 and those Canadians who succumbed to their wounds we buried in a number of cemeteries in France and the United Kingdom. The list below contains the predominant cemeteries where these men are buried.

FAUBOURG D'AMIENS CEMETERY, Arras

The cemetery is located in southeastern part of the city. It was made by fighting units and field ambulances in 1916.

It now contains the graves of 2,652 Commonwealth soldiers of which 152 are Canadian.

The burials are predominantly those of Canadians who succumbed to their wounds received in the Battles of Arras 1918 and the Drocourt-Queant line.

Surrounding the entrance to the cemetery is the Arras Memorial to the Missing for British and South African soldiers who died in the Battle of Arras 1917 and the defense of Arras 1918 and have no known grave. Over 35,000 names are engraved on the walls. At the centre of the memorial is a second memorial column to the missing of the Air Services. Surmounted by a globe the 4 sides of the memorial have the names of 1,018 missing airmen. 47 are directly attributed to Canada although many others were also Canadian.

Two Victoria Cross winners, Major Lanoe Hawker, VC, DSO, Royal Flying Corps (the Red Baron's 10th victim) and Major Mick Mannock, VC, DSO and 2 bars, MC and bar, of the Royal Air Force, the British Ace of Aces with 73 kills, top two of the panels.

AUBIGNY COMMUNAL CEMETERY EXTENSION

The Cemetery is located south of the village, which is just north of the main Arras-St. Pol Road, 20 kms west of Arras.

It was made by Casualty Clearing Stations from 1916 to 1918.

It contains the graves of 2,771 Commonwealth soldiers of which 666 are Canadian. The Canadians buried here reflect the actions throughout their stay on the Arras front from 1916, through the battles of Vimy Ridge and Arras 1918.

Private Claude Patrick Nunney, VC, DCM, MM, 38th Battalion (Eastern Ontario) is buried in Plot IV, Row B, Grave 39. Nunney won his Victoria Cross of the night of 1/2 September 1918 near Vis-en-Artois, greatly assisting in repelling a German counterattack.

LIGNY-ST. FLOCHEL BRITISH CEMETERY

The cemetery is located south-west of the village which is 20 km north-west of Arras on the Arras-St.Pol road.

The cemetery was made in April 1918 by the 33rd Casualty Clearing Station.

It contains the graves of 632 Commonwealth soldiers including 348 Canadians (1 is unidentified). The Canadians buried here are predominantly those who were mortally wounded in the Battle of Arras 1918 and the Drocourt-Queant line. Men of all units of the 4 Canadian Divisions and supporting troops are buried here.

Along the coast north and south of Boulogne there are 2 hospital centre cemeteries which contain a number of Canadians mortally wounded at Arras and the D-Q line 1918.

ETAPLES MILITARY CEMETERY

Etaples Cemetery is on the coastal road between Boulogne and Le Treport, three kilometers north of Etaples. It was used through-

Howard Herbert Farley
Private
14th (Royal Montreal) Battalion
Killed in action September 2, 1918.
Born at New Haven, Connecticut, December 6th, 1896. He was the son of Mr. and Mrs. H.T. Farley of Outremont, Quebec. Student at McGill University.
Enlisted at Richmond, Quebec, July 19th, 1917 in the 258th Battalion.
During military operations on September 2nd, 1918 against the Drocourt-Queant line, near Cagnicourt he was killed by the enemy. No further details are available. His body was recovered from the battlefield in 1919 and was reburied in Queant Road Cemetery, Buissy.

Francis Michael Murphy
Lieutenant
15th - 48th Highlanders
Died of wounds September 2, 1918
Born at Carleton Place, Ontario, June 30th, 1887. Son of James Murphy.
Enlisted at Toronto, December 1915. Transferred, as a Lieutenant to the 15th Battalion in 1918 and went to France.
While taking part with his Battalion in the attack on the Drocourt-Queant line he was hit in the stomach by a machine gun bullet about 9:00 a.m. on September 2nd, 1918 and died the same day at No. 2 Canadian Field Ambulance. He is buried in Anzin-St. Aubin British Cemetery near Arras.

out the war and contains 10,729 Commonwealth graves, including 1,123 Canadians. This cemetery reflects the Canadian losses during the major actions of Mount Sorrel, the Somme, Vimy, Passchendaele and the Advance to Victory.

Etaples was the major depot base for the British army on the Western Front and was the location of the infamous Bull Ring and the British mutiny of 1917.

On May 19, 1918, German Gotha bombers made direct hits on the No. 1 Canadian General hospital, killing 66 people, including three nursing sisters. The men killed in the attack are buried in Plots 66, 67 and 68. The nursing sisters are buried in Plot 28.

TERLINCTHUN MILITARY CEMETERY, Wimille

The cemetery is located within view of the English Channel 4 km north of Boulogne.

It was opened in the summer of 1918 when the existing cemeteries at Boulogne Eastern and Wimereux Communal were filled. It was used by hospitals in the vicinity. The cemetery is still open for burials and receives the remains found today in fields and villages of France. Even after 80 years the skeletons of the Great War still surface. There are an estimated 110,000 Commonwealth soldiers whose remains have yet to be recovered.

It contains the graves of 4,338 Commonwealth soldiers of which 316 are Canadian (27 are unidentified).

In 1922 when the cemetery was first closed it contained 3,011 burials of which 277 were Canadian. Since that time more than 1,300 bodies have been found and reburied here. Some have been identified.

The last "identified" Canadian burial took place in 1987 when the remains of Private John Willoughby of the Lord Strathcona's Horse were found in Moreuil Wood. He was killed there 30 March 1918. In 1976 the identified remains (including his pipe) of Private George Coker of the 4th Battalion Canadian Mounted Rifles (Toronto) were found near Vimy. He was killed 21 April 1917.

Carl Gordon Laberee
Lieutenant
87th Montreal Grenadier Guards
Died of wounds November 28,1918.
Born at Sawyerville, Quebec, October
19th, 1896. Youngest son of Henry
and Alice Laberee of Lennoxville,
Quebec.
Enlisted in the 87th Battalion at
Montreal in 1915. Commissioned as
a Lieutenant in January 1918.
On the early morning of September
2nd, 1918 at Mont Dury, while lying
in No Man's land with his platoon he
was severely wounded by enemy
shell-fire. He was evacuated to
England where he succumbed to his
wounds two months later. Buried in
Brookwood Cemetery, Surrey,
England.

Eric Drummond-Hay
Lieutenant
16th Canadian Scottish
Killed in action September 2, 1918.
Born at Belmont, Manitoba,
November 26th, 1896. Son of
Edward Drummond-Hay of Kitscoty,
Alberta. Enlisted in 1915, before he
was 18: promoted Lieutenant, 1918.
During the early stages of the attack
on the Drocourt-Queant line,
September 2nd, 1918 he was
wounded in the arm when leading his
men. While proceeding to the
Dressing Station he was shot through
the head by an enemy sniper and
killed. His older brother, Leonard
Vivian, was killed 19 days earlier at
Parvillers, near Amiens..

THE NEWFOUNDLANDERS

Throughout the Western front there are hundreds of memorials scattered in the fields and villages marking heroic exploits. Some commemorate the sacrifice of Divisions or Regiments while others mark the battles won by the Dominions of the British Empire, the Young Lions. These are touching Memorials to the Canadians, Australians, New Zealanders and South Africans who perished on the Western front. It is always moving to observe these tributes to men from far lands who came to France to die. None of them are as poignant as the solitary bronze Caribou that marks the sacrifices of the Men of Newfoundland.

Newfoundland was Britain's smallest lion when war was declared in 1914. But like all others across the Empire the call of the Mother Country could not be refused and Newfoundlanders enthusiastically enlisted. Proud of their heritage, which was distinctly not Canadian, they formed their own Regiment and served with distinction from 1915 to 1918. They were the only Regiment who earned the King's title of "Royal" during the entire war.

The 1st Battalion, the Royal Newfoundland Regiment, served with British Divisions throughout the War. They first fought at Gallipoli in 1915, and were fortunate in escaping the bloody battles on the peninsula. After the campaign ended they came to France virtually intact. In France the Newfoundlanders' luck ran out and in the battles that followed suffered enormous casualties. It seemed each time they were committed, everything went wrong.

Their first battle in France was on the disastrous July 1st, 1916 when in less than one hour they suffered more than 700 casualties including 300 dead. This catastrophic attack even failed to reach the German wire!

The next action on the Somme was reasonable successful when the Newfoundlanders captured a series of trenches near Guedecourt. The cost was 120 dead.

In the Battle of Arras, 1917, the Newfoundland Regiment attacked just east of Monchy-le-Preux. The Germans cut off the exposed Regiment and inflicted 300 casualties and took 153 prisoners.

The next major battle for the Newfoundlanders was in the first great Tank attack in history, in the Battle of Cambrai.

The Newfoundland Caribou (Beaumont-Hamel Newfoundland Memorial).
(PHOTO: N. CHRISTIE)

On November 20th, 1917, they attacked near Masnieres and rode the wave of success of the British tanks. The Germans counter-attacked on November 30th, regaining almost all the lost ground . The Battle of Cambrai cost the Regiment more than 400 killed, wounded and missing.

By the end of the War one in four of the 6000 Newfoundlanders who served had died. It was a crushing sacrifice for the small communities of the Island, and the worst proportionate losses of any of the countries of the Empire.

To honour their dead, the Government of Newfoundland purchased 5 sites to honour their major battles. Each was marked with Basil Gotto's beautiful, bronze Caribou, so distinctively of Newfoundland, staring in the direction of the enemy. No description accompanies the statues and none seems necessary. They are powerful, yet sad reminders of the poor lads who came so far to die for King and Empire.

The Caribou stands watch over the old battlefields at:

Beaumont-Hamel, on the Somme. *It marks the sacrifice of the Newfoundland Regiment on July 1st, 1916. It is placed in the most impressive Park on the Western Front.*

Guedecourt, on the Somme. *The Caribou sits in a small park and marks their successful advance in the Battle of Le Transloy, October 12th, 1916.*

Monchy-le-Preux, east of Arras. *The Caribou is in the centre of the village and commemorates the action in the Battle of Arras, April 14th, 1917.*

Masnieres, south-west of Cambrai. *This park is in the village and marks the action of the Newfoundlanders in the Battle of Cambrai, November 20th-30th, 1917.*

Courtrai (Kortrijk), Belgium. *This site honours the attack of the Newfoundlanders in the advance to victory, October 14th-20th, 1918.*

CONSCRIPTION

In the early morning of August 26th, 1918, the 2nd Canadian Mounted Rifles launched an attack against the German trenches on Orange Hill. Their attack was successful and the 2nd CMR advanced quickly with light casualties.

Private William Johnson was in that initial attack and the pursuit to Monchy. In the confusion of battle Johnson and 2 comrades went a short distance beyond the objective. The 3 took shelter in a shell-hole to avoid machine-gun fire but Johnson's head was exposed and a bullet passed through his forehead, killing him instantly.

William Douglas Johnson was born in Bracebridge, Ontario, in 1897; the son of Thomas and Amelia Johnson. In 1917 he was attended Law School before he joined the Colours. William Johnson had arrived in France on August 15th, 1918. His contribution to the Great War lasted only 11 days!

In many ways William Johnson was no different than the 50,000 Canadian soldiers who had died before him. He was 5'4 1/2", a Methodist and clearly the son of proud parents. But William Johnson was quite different. He was not a volunteer, he was a conscript.

Few issues in Canadian politics have been as divisive as Conscription. The First World War had drawn hundreds of thousand of volunteers but still many Canadian-born men were not drawn to the attraction of the War. The first contingents had been predominantly British-born and Canada's manpower contribution to the War effort was proportionately lower than Britain, Australia, and New Zealand.

The Canadian Prime Minister, Sir Robert Borden, had visited the Canadian Corps in March 1917. He was, at that time, staunchly against Conscription but Borden had been convinced by the faces of the Canadian soldiers in France that more help was needed. On his return to Canada Borden set to work on the Military Service Act, to raise 100,000 more men for the Canadian Corps. His Conscription bill was opposed by the opposition Liberals, and Borden was forced to call a General Election.

The issue was clearly a problem. Not only had English-Canadians not responded like the other countries of the Empire,

The grave of William Johnson, killed in action August 26, 1918.

(PHOTO: N. CHRISTIE)

they resented French-Canada for responding even less. Borden then made the divisive issue even worse by trying to fix the election by disenfranchising some Canadians, enfranchising others and allowing any Canadian soldier overseas to cast votes in any Constituency. Borden's manipulations were not necessary as he won an overwhelming majority.

In August, 1917, The Military Service Act had called for the registration of all eligible men. They were divided into 6 classes from Class 1, unmarried men between the ages of 20 and 45, to Class 6, married men between the ages of 40-44.

By the end of all the wrangling and bureaucratic moves, 400,000 Class 1 men were registered; 220,000 of these were exempted from service and 24,000 defaulted. The net result was 100,000 men were taken on strength in the Canadian Forces; 47,000 went overseas but only 24,000 went to France before the Armistice.

The first conscripts arrived in mid-August 1918 and were quickly sent in to reinforce the front line battalions after their losses at Amiens and Arras. One of those men was William Douglas Johnson.

His headstone in Monchy British Cemetery bears the high service number (3033865) characteristic of many of the MSA men. A poignant inscription at the base of his headstone marks his memory, one of the first conscripts to die;

"FAITHFUL UNTO DEATH."

THE KAISER'S DESPAIR

Realizing That the End is Near, He Makes His Will

(FROM OUR SPECIAL CORRESPONDENT IN BERLIN)

It is rumored in Germany that the Emperor now realizes that his number is up and is accordingly making his Will, revoking all Wills made heretofore.

This Will is said to read as follows:

This is the Last Will and Testament of me, Wilhelm, the super-swanker and ruler of the sausage eaters, recognizing that I am fairly up against it and expecting to meet with a violent death at any minute at the hands of the brave Canadians, hereby make my last Will and Testament.

I appoint the Emperor of Austria to be my sole executor (by kind permission of the Allies.)

1. I give and bequeath to France, the territories of Alsace and Lorraine (as this is only a case of returning stolen property, I don't deserve any credit for it, and am not likely to get any, either.)

2. To Servia I give Austria.

3. To Russia I give Turkey, for the Czar's Christmas Dinner.

4. To Belgium I should like to give all the thick ears, black eyes and broken noses that she presented me with when I politely trespassed on her territory.

5. To the Land of the Maple I give all my Dreadnaughts, Submarines, Torpedo Boat Destroyers and Fleet of Flunkers generally, what's left of them. They are bound to have them in the end, so this is only anticipating events.

6. Also I give what's left of my army as Currie and his MEN are so handy at turning my men into sausage meat.

7. To the College of Science and Museum I leave my famous moustaches, souvenir of the greatest swanker in this or any other age.

8. To Mrs. Pankhurst and the wild women I leave my mailed fist; they'll find it useful, no doubt, when they resume their Militant tactics.

9. To Sir Ernest Shackleton I leave the pole; I've been up it so long that I regard it as my personal property.

(Signed) H.I.M. WILHELM
Lord of the Land, Sea and Air,
Not forgetting the Sausages and Lager Beer.

Signed by the above named WILHELM as his last Will in the presence of us, his ministers and keepers, present at the same time, who in his presence and in the presence of each other, hath hereunto subscribed their names as witnesses.

BARON VON SAUERKRAUT.
GRAF VON MUNICHLAGERBIER.

Propoganda. The Kaiser's Will according to the Canadian Corps.

The Dawn of Peace

I've been reading the Pope's peaceful messages,
Sent out to the Nations from Rome,
Was considering the losses and suffering,
Of our loved ones abroad and at home.
In my old armchair I sat thinking,
Alone by the firelight gleam,
Until the Chains of slumber found me,
And I had a wierd, strange dream.
I looked down on a desolate valley,
Amid ruins and smoke and mud,
I saw thousands of shattered homesteads,
And a winding river of blood.
Down in that desert valley,
It was as deep as a mountain pass,
Crimson, shattered, torn and blistered,
It looked like the Mouth of Hell.
From below came the roar of cannon,
And the fumes of poisonous gas,
I noticed the gaunt-like features,
Slowly climbing a desert pass.
Around him were threatening shadows,
From which he vainly sought release,
Then I caught a glimplse of his features,
It was the Kaiser looking for peace.
Madly begging the God of the Germans,
To uphold his name and race,
When the Devil flew out from the shadows,
And laughed in the tyrant's face.
"What you master of evil,
King of the Huns,
After training your millions of soldiers,
And constructing your giant guns.
Come now, think how you fooled the English,
When they ceded you Heligoland,
And remember your promises of friendship,
When you gave them your withered hand.
And why did you build such a Navy,
Then boast of your might and your worth,

Was it simply for peace that you did it,
No you were greedy and wanted the Earth.
That is why you invaded Belgium,
Commanded your Huns to destroy, to burn,
Rape and shoot without mercy,
Why you gazed on the scene in joy,
While even I cannot count the victims,
That you've murdered on land and the waves,
But men will remember Nurse Cavell,
Who you sent to a martyr's grave.
And they will curse you for shooting brave Fryatt,
While your body lies cold and still,
You may try to forget that murder,
But history never will.
Were you thinking of peace,
When you ordered your Zepps and your planes,
To creep over peaceful city and Hamlet,
And murder women and babes in their sleep.
Was it peace that made your submarine pirates,
Sink innocent souls 'neath the flood,
Why through you both the land and the ocean,
Have been crimson with human blood.
Now you've callen your God for protection,
Begged for peace like a cowardly Nave,
But the peace that you get is not heaven,
It's down in the Hell that you've made.
To its bottomless depth you will travel,
Amid torments that never shall cease,
And the flaming tongues that scorch you,
Will herald the Dawn of Peace.

The "Dawn of Peace" was recited to the author in 1985 by Cecil Palmer, a veteran of the Great War. At the time, Cecil was 90 years old, and still worked on his farm in Wharncliffe, Ontario. He served as a sniper with the 102nd Battalion, and was wounded October 31st, 1917 at Passchendaele and again September 2, 1918 at the Drocourt-Queant line. Cecil Palmer died at Thessalon, Ontario, April, 1990.

FOR FURTHER REFERENCE

The Battle of Arras 1918 and the Drocourt-Queant line was the greatest victory of the Canadian Corps in the First World War. However the record of the Canadians was distinguished from 1915 to 1918 and although this book has solely focused on the one battle there is much more to Canadian battles of the Great War. In addition the Great War for Civilization has left many reminders of the sacrifice of British, French, Australian and German troops on the Western Front. Much is worth seeing.

Below I have outlined a number of guidebooks which will assist in the understanding of and visits to the Great War battlefields on the Western Front. A list of general books which would also assist is also presented below. Sadly there is very little on the Canadian victories (or the Allied ones for that matter) in 1918.

BATTLE GUIDES

Before Endeavours Fade, by R.E. Coombs. Battle of Britain Prints International, 1976.

The Somme Battlefields, by M. And M. Middlebrook. Viking 1981.

The Somme Then and Now, by J. Giles. Battle of Britain Prints International, 1986.

The Western Front, Then and Now, by J. Giles. Battle of Britain Prints, 1992.

THE ADVANCE TO VICTORY

The Official History of the Canadian Expeditionary Force 1914-19, by G.W.L. Nicholson. The Queen's Printer, 1962.

Canada's Hundred Days, by J.F.B. Livesay. Thomas Allen, 1919.

Spearhead to Victory, by D. Dancocks. Hurtig Publishers, 1987.

A Wood Called Bourlon, by William Moore. Leo Cooper, 1988.

With the Canadian Army Medical Corps in the Last Hundred Days, by A.E. Snell. F.A. Ackland 1924.

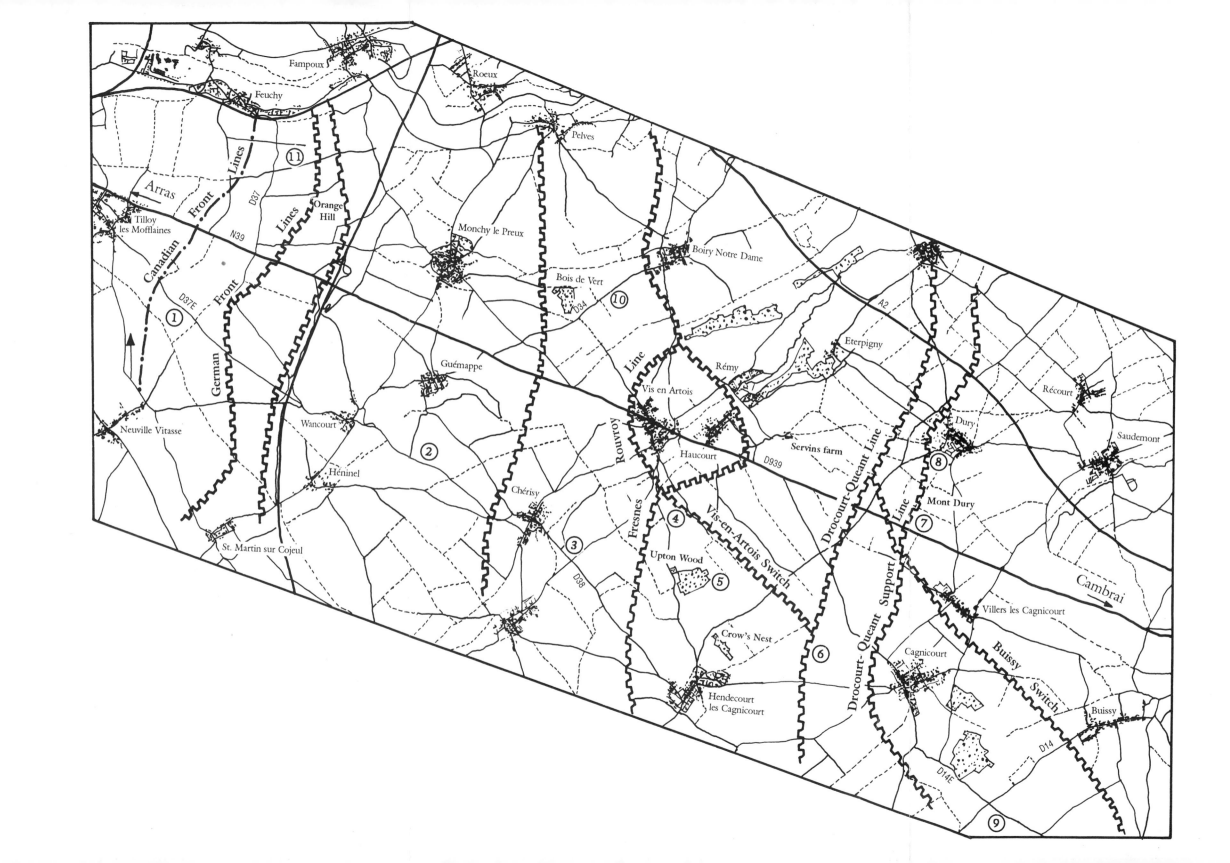